CCAT 4 WORKBOOK

Canadian Cognitive Abilities
Test - Grade 4 - Level 10

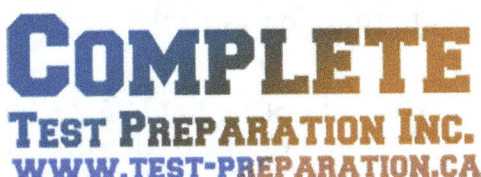

Copyright

Copyright © 2025 by Complete Test Preparation Inc.

ALL RIGHTS RESERVED.

No part of this book may be reproduced or transferred in any form or by any means, graphic, electronic, or mechanical, including photocopying, recording, web distribution, taping, or by any information storage retrieval system, without the written permission of the author.

Notice: Complete Test Preparation Inc. makes every reasonable effort to obtain from reliable sources accurate, complete, and timely information about the tests covered in this book. Nevertheless, changes can be made in the tests or the administration of the tests at any time and Complete Test Preparation Inc. makes no representation or warranty, either expressed or implied as to the accuracy, timeliness, or completeness of the information contained in this book. Complete Test Preparation Inc. make no representations or warranties of any kind, express or implied, about the completeness, accuracy, reliability, suitability or availability with respect to the information contained in this document for any purpose. Any reliance you place on such information is therefore strictly at your own risk.

The author(s) shall not be liable for any loss incurred as a consequence of the use and application, directly or indirectly, of any information presented in this work. Sold with the understanding, the author is not engaged in rendering professional services or advice. If advice or expert assistance is required, the services of a competent professional should be sought.

The company, product and service names used in this publication are for identification purposes only. All trademarks and registered trademarks are the property of their respective owners. Complete Test Preparation Inc. is not affiliated with any educational institution.

The producers and administrators of the CCAT are not involved in the production of, and does not endorse this publication.

This title is provided for skill practice only.

We strongly recommend that students check with exam providers for up-to-date information regarding test content.

Version 9.0 February 2024

ISBN: 9781772454642

About Complete Test Preparation Inc.

Why Us?
The Complete Test Preparation Team has been publishing high quality study materials since 2005, with a catalogue of over 145 titles, in English, French and Chinese, as well as curriculum for all levels.

To keep up with the industry changes, we update everything all the time!

And the best part?
With every purchase, you're helping people all over the world improve themselves and their education. So thank you in advance for supporting this mission with us! Together, we are truly making a difference in the lives of those often forgotten by the system.

Charities that we support - https://www.test-preparation.ca/charities-and-non-profits/

You have definitely come to the right place.
If you want to spend your valuable study time where it will help you the most - we've got you covered today and tomorrow.

Published by
Complete Test Preparation Inc.
Victoria BC Canada

Visit us on the web at
https://www.test-preparation.ca
Printed in the USA

FEEDBACK

We welcome your feedback. Email us at feedback@test-preparation.ca with your comments and suggestions. We carefully review all suggestions and often incorporate reader suggestions into upcoming versions. As a Print on Demand Publisher, we update our products frequently.

CONTENTS

8 Introduction
10 Verbal Battery

    Vocabulary Quiz I   14
    Answer Key   24

    Vocabulary Quiz 2   28
    Answer Key   40

    Sentence Completion   44
    Answer Key   53

    Analogies Quiz   59
    Answer Key   70

    Analogies Quiz 2   72
    Answer Key   82

83 Non Verbal Battery

    Classification Quiz   86
    Answer Key   96

    Classification Quiz 2   99
    Answer Key   108

    Folding Quiz   113
    Answer Key   123

    Folding Quiz 2   125
    Answer Key   135

    Figure Matrix Quiz   139
    Answer Key   149

Number Analogies Quiz	155
Answer Key	163
Number Series Quiz 1	171
Answer Key	181
Number Series Quiz 2	185
Answer Key	195
Number Puzzles Quiz	200
Answer Key	208

209 Taking a Practice Test
Getting the Most from Practice	210
After Completing a Practice Test	211

213 Test Preparation Tips
214 How to Answer Multiple Choice
217 Conclusion

INTRODUCTION

Welcome to the Canadian Cognitive Abilities Test Practice Workbook. This resource is designed to help you prepare your child for assessments that evaluate reasoning and problem-solving skills across three key areas:

Verbal Battery: Enhances language comprehension and verbal reasoning abilities.

Quantitative Battery: Develops numerical reasoning and problem-solving skills.

Non-Verbal Battery: Strengthens your ability to understand and analyze visual information.

By working through the practice questions in this workbook with your child, you'll build confidence and proficiency in each area.

Engaging with your Grade 4 child using a practice workbook can be a rewarding experience that reinforces their learning and fosters a positive attitude toward education. Here are some guidelines to help you make the most of this time together:

Establish a Routine: Set aside a consistent time each day for workbook activities. A regular schedule helps your child develop good study habits and provides a sense of structure.

Create a Conducive Environment: Ensure that the study area is quiet, well-lit, and free from distractions. A comfortable space can enhance concentration and make learning more enjoyable.

Review Instructions Together: Before starting an exercise, read the instructions with your child to make sure they understand the questions. Generally it is self explanatory, but reviewing will not hurt! Encourage them to ask questions if anything is unclear.

Encourage Independence: Allow your child to attempt the exercises on their own first. This promotes problem-solving skills and confidence. Offer guidance only when necessary, and praise successful efforts to build self-esteem and confidence.

Discuss Mistakes Positively: Mistakes are learning opportunities. Discuss what went wrong and how to approach similar problems differently in the future. This fosters a growth and problem-solving as well as building confidence.

Use Real-Life Examples: Relate workbook questions to everyday situations. This makes learning relevant and practical.

Celebrate Achievements: Acknowledge your child's progress and successes, no matter how small. Positive reinforcement encourages continued effort and enthusiasm for learning.

These are just a few steps you can take to create a supportive and effective learning environment that complements your child's educational journey.

Verbal Battery Vocabulary I

The Verbal Battery vocabulary section of the Canadian Cognitive Abilities Test (CCAT) for grade 4 evaluates a student's understanding and use of language.

This section includes questions that test vocabulary, verbal analogies, sentence completion, and comprehension skills. Students are asked to demonstrate their knowledge of word meanings, relationships between words, and their ability to follow and interpret written instructions or passages. The goal is to measure a student's linguistic aptitude, which is important for success in various academic subjects.

For example, a vocabulary question might ask students to choose the word that best completes a sentence, while a verbal analogy question might ask them to identify the relationship between pairs of words. Sentence completion questions require students to select the best word to fill in a blank in a sentence, and comprehension questions assess their ability to understand and interpret written passages.

Tips for Answering Vocabulary Questions

1. Understand the Word:

Make sure you know the meaning of the word. For example, if the word is "brave," understand that it means showing courage.

2. Use Context Clues:

Look at the words around the unfamiliar word to help figure out its meaning. For example, in the sentence "The brave knight fought the dragon," the word "fought" can help you understand that "brave" means courageous.

3. Break Down the Word:

Look for smaller words or familiar parts within the word. For example, in the word "unhappy," you can see "happy" and know that "un-" means not, so "unhappy" means not happy.

4. Think of Synonyms and Antonyms:

Think of words that mean the same or the opposite. For example, a synonym for "happy" is "joyful," and an antonym is "sad."

5. Practice with Flashcards:

Use flashcards to review vocabulary words. Write the word on one side and the definition on the other. For example, write "brave" on one side and "showing courage" on the other.

6. Use the Word in a Sentence:

Practice using the word in a sentence to understand its meaning better. For example, "The brave firefighter saved the cat from the tree."

8. Ask for Help:

If you don't understand a word, ask a teacher, parent, or friend for help. For example, if you don't know what "giggle" means, ask someone to explain it to you.

9. Stay Calm and Focused:

Take your time and stay calm when answering questions. For example, if you come across a difficult word, take a deep breath and use the strategies you've learned.

Quiz 1 Answer Sheet

	A	B	C	D	E		A	B	C	D	E
1	○	○	○	○	○	21	○	○	○	○	○
2	○	○	○	○	○	22	○	○	○	○	○
3	○	○	○	○	○	23	○	○	○	○	○
4	○	○	○	○	○	24	○	○	○	○	○
5	○	○	○	○	○	25	○	○	○	○	○
6	○	○	○	○	○	26	○	○	○	○	○
7	○	○	○	○	○	27	○	○	○	○	○
8	○	○	○	○	○	28	○	○	○	○	○
9	○	○	○	○	○	29	○	○	○	○	○
10	○	○	○	○	○	30	○	○	○	○	○
11	○	○	○	○	○						
12	○	○	○	○	○						
13	○	○	○	○	○						
14	○	○	○	○	○						
15	○	○	○	○	○						
16	○	○	○	○	○						
17	○	○	○	○	○						
18	○	○	○	○	○						
19	○	○	○	○	○						
20	○	○	○	○	○						

1. What is the definition of 'polygon?'

   A. A curved line
   B. A straight line
   C. A closed plane figure with straight sides
   D. A round shape

2. Which term means to 'depict or show something?'

   A. Represent   B. Cause
   C. Infer   D. Estimate

3. What is the synonym for 'trigger?'

   A. Polygon   B. Represent
   C. Cause   D. Infer

4. What does it mean to 'deduce or conclude from evidence and reasoning?'

    A. Polygon   B. Represent
    C. Cause   D. Infer

5. To 'roughly calculate or judge the value or extent of something' is to:

    A. Polygon   B. Represent
    C. Cause   D. Estimate

6. What does 'adaptation' mean?
    A. A type of food
    B. A change or adjustment to fit new circumstances
    C. A unit of measure
    D. A piece of furniture

7. Which word means a collection of maps in book form?

    A. Adaptation   B. Atlas
    C. Multiply   D. Automatic

8. What is the meaning of the word 'multiply?'

    A. To subtract B. To add
    C. To divide
    D. To increase in number or amount

9. Which word best describes something that operates by itself with little human intervention?

    A. Adaptation   B. Atlas
    C. Multiply   D. Automatic

10. What does it mean to 'persuade' someone?

    A. To confuse   B. To force
    C. To convince or influence
    D. To delay

11. Which word means 'a change that is a result or consequence of an action or other cause?'

    A. Effect   B. Confirm
    C. Except   D. Maximum

12. Which word means 'to establish the truth, accuracy, or validity of something?'

    A. Effect   B. Confirm
    C. Except   D. Maximum

13. Which word means 'not including; other than?'

    A. Effect   B. Confirm
    C. Except   D. Maximum

14. Which word means 'the greatest quantity or value attainable or attainable under given circumstances?'

    A. Effect   B. Confirm
    C. Except   D. Maximum

15. Which word means 'outcome or consequence of an action, event, or situation?'

    A. Effect   B. Confirm
    C. Except   D. Maximum

16. Which word means to give a brief statement of the main points of something?

    A. Summarize B. Recommend
    C. Minimum   D. Accomplish

17. Which word means to suggest or endorse something as being good or suitable?

    A. Summarize B. Recommend
    C. Minimum   D. Accomplish

18. Which word refers to the smallest amount possible or allowable?

    A. Summarize B. Recommend
    C. Minimum   D. Accomplish

19. Which word means to achieve or complete something successfully?

    A. Summarize   B. Recommend
    C. Minimum   D. Accomplish

20. Which word refers to the reason for which something is done or created?

    A. Summarize   B. Recommend
    C. Minimum   D. Accomplish

21. Which word means to make a deep sound indicating pain or displeasure?

    A. groan   B. loan
    C. rowed   D. creek

22. Which word refers to a sum of money that is borrowed?

    A. groan   B. loan
    C. rowed   D. creek

23. Which word means to propel a boat through water using oars?

    A. groan   B. loan
    C. rowed   D. creek

24. Which word refers to a small stream or brook?

    A. groan   B. loan
    C. rowed   D. creek

25. Which word describes a way or course taken in getting from a starting point to a destination?

   A. groan
   B. loan
   C. rowed
   D. creek

26. Which word means old and no longer fresh or new?

   A. stale
   B. float
   B. fresh
   C. sink

27. Which word means to remain on the surface of a liquid without sinking?

   A. stale
   B. float
   B. fresh
   C. sink

28. Which word means recently made, produced, or harvested?

    A. stale   B. float
    B. fresh   C. sink

29. Which word means to go down below the surface of water, mud, etc.?

    A. stale   B. float
    B. fresh   C. sink

30. Which word means no longer alive?

    A. stale   B. float
    C. fresh   D. dead

Answer Key

1. C
A polygon is a closed plane figure with straight sides, such as a triangle, square, or pentagon.

2. A
'Represent' means to depict or show something through symbols, images, or actions.

3. C
'Cause' is a synonym for trigger, as it refers to something that produces an effect or result.

4 D
'Infer' means to deduce or conclude from evidence and reasoning, often by interpreting implicit information.

5 D
'Estimate' means to roughly calculate or judge the value or extent of something based on available information or experience.

6. B
'Adaptation' refers to a change or adjustment to fit new circumstances or environment.

7. B
'Atlas' is a collection of maps in book form.

8. D
'Multiply' means to increase in number or amount.

9. D
'Automatic' means operating by itself with little human intervention.

10. C
'Persuade' means to convince or influence someone to do or believe something.

11. A
'Effect' because 'effect' refers to the result or consequence of an action.

12. B
Confirm' because 'confirm' means to establish the truth, accuracy, or validity of something.

13. C
'Except' because 'except' means not including; other than.

14. D
'Maximum' because it refers to the greatest quantity or value attainable.

15. A
'Effect' because it refers to the outcome or consequence of an action, event, or situation.

16. A
Summarize' as it means to provide a concise overview of the main points or ideas of something.

17. B
'Recommend' as it refers to advising or suggesting something as being desirable or appropriate.

18. C
'Minimum' as it denotes the lowest quantity, degree, or extent that is possible or required.

19. D
'Accomplish' as it means to successfully complete a task or goal.

20. D
'Purpose' as it signifies the intention or objective behind an action or existence of something.

21. A
'Groan.' To groan means to make a deep, involuntary sound indicating pain or discomfort.

22. B
'Loan.' A loan is a sum of money that is borrowed with the expectation of repayment.

23. C
'Rowed.' Rowed means to propel a boat through water using oars or rowing equipment.

24. D
'Creek.' A creek is a small stream or brook that flows into a larger body of water.

25. D
'Route.' A route is a way or course taken to get from a starting point to a destination.

26. A
'Stale' as it is defined as old and no longer fresh or new.

27. B
'Float' which means to remain on the surface of a liquid without sinking.

28. C
'Fresh' as it means recently made, produced, or harvested.

29. D
'Sink' which means to go down below the surface of water, mud, etc.

30. D
'Dead' which means no longer alive.

Vocabulary Quiz 2

Answer Sheet

	A	B	C	D	E		A	B	C	D	E
1	○	○	○	○	○	21	○	○	○	○	○
2	○	○	○	○	○	22	○	○	○	○	○
3	○	○	○	○	○	23	○	○	○	○	○
4	○	○	○	○	○	24	○	○	○	○	○
5	○	○	○	○	○	25	○	○	○	○	○
6	○	○	○	○	○	26	○	○	○	○	○
7	○	○	○	○	○	27	○	○	○	○	○
8	○	○	○	○	○	28	○	○	○	○	○
9	○	○	○	○	○	29	○	○	○	○	○
10	○	○	○	○	○	30	○	○	○	○	○
11	○	○	○	○	○						
12	○	○	○	○	○						
13	○	○	○	○	○						
14	○	○	○	○	○						
15	○	○	○	○	○						
16	○	○	○	○	○						
17	○	○	○	○	○						
18	○	○	○	○	○						
19	○	○	○	○	○						
20	○	○	○	○	○						

1. What does 'accurate' mean?

   A. Precise
   B. Careless
   C. Flexible
   D. Simple

2. Which word means to examine something closely and in detail?

   A. Analyze
   B. Burrow
   C. Coax
   D. Carefree

3. What does 'burrow' mean?

   A. To dig a hole
   B. To fly high
   C. To swim fast
   D. To climb a tree

4. Which word describes a person who is cheerful and without worries?

    A. Carefree   B. Analyze
    C. Coax   D. Accurate

5. What does it mean to 'coax' someone?

    A. To persuade gently
    B. To shout loudly
    C. To jump high
    D. To sleep deeply

6. What does 'communicate' mean?

    A. To destroy   B. To conclude
    C. To craft
    D. To convey information

7. Which word is the opposite of 'constructive?'

    A. Crafty   B. Conclude
    C. Destructive D. Disaster

8. What does 'conclude' mean?

    A. To create   B. Communicate
    C. To finish   D. To destroy

9. Which word best describes someone who is sly and clever in a deceptive way?

    A. Communicate B. Conclude
    C. Crafty   D. Destructive

10. What does 'disaster' mean?

   A. Construct   B. Communicate
   C. A great success
   D. A sudden event causing widespread destruction

11. Which word means 'whole or complete?'

   A. Entire   B. Envy
   C. Fragile   D. Frequent

12. Which word means 'a feeling of discontented longing inspired by someone else's possessions?'

   A. Entire   B. Envy
   C. Fragile   D. Frequent

13. Which word means 'easily broken or damaged?'

    A. Entire   B. Envy
    C. Fragile   D. Frequent

14. Which word means 'happening often or at short intervals?'

    A. Entire   B. Envy
    C. Fragile   D. Frequent

15. Which word means 'having or showing a modest or low estimate of one's importance?'

    A. Entire   B. Envy
    C. Fragile   D. Humble

16. What is the meaning of the word 'impact?'

    A. Light   B. Influence
    C. Silence   D. Question

17. Which word means to be fully developed and grown?

    A. Childish   B. Immature
    C. Mature   D. Junior

18. What does 'mistrust' mean?

    A. Trust   B. Fear
    C. Suspicion D. Respect

19. Which word describes something exceptional or excellent?

    A. Average   B. Good
    C. Outstanding D. Common

20. What do we call someone who is of the same age group or social standing?

    A. Mentor   B. Superior
    C. Elder   D. Peer

21. Which word means to like something more than other things?

    A. Prefer   B. Queasy
    C. Reduce   D. Resist

22. Which word means feeling sick or nauseated?

    A. Reduce   B. Queasy
    C. Resist   D. Reveal

23. Which word means to make something smaller in size, amount, or number?

    A. Resist   B. Reduce
    C. Reveal   D. Refer

24. Which word means to try to stop or avoid something?

    A. Resist   B. Prefer
    C. Queasy   D. Reveal

25. Which word means to make something known or visible that was previously hidden or secret?

    A. Reduce   B. Reveal
    C. Prefer   D. Queasy

26. Which word means 'worn out and shabby?'

    A. Sole   B. Shabby
    C. Sturdy   D. Tradition

27. What does 'sole' mean?

    A. Only   B. Sturdy
    C. Tradition   D. Variety

28. Which word means 'strong and robust?'

    A. Sturdy   B. Tradition
    C. Variety   D. Shabby

29. What does 'tradition' refer to?

    A. Sturdy   B. Old practice
    C. Variety   D. Shabby

30. Which word means 'a range of different things?'

    A. Sturdy   B. Tradition
    C. Variety   D. Shabby

Answer Key

1. A
'Accurate' means precise, correct, or exact. It is the best choice that matches the meaning of the word.

2. A
'Analyze' means to examine something in detail. It is the most appropriate choice that aligns with the word's definition.

3. A
'Burrow' means to dig a hole or tunnel. It is the most relevant option corresponding to the word's meaning.

4. A
'Carefree' means having no worries or anxieties. It is the most fitting choice based on the word's definition.

5. A
'Coax' means to persuade or urge gently. It is the most suitable option reflecting the word's definition.

6. D
To convey information' because 'communicate' means to exchange thoughts, ideas, or information with others.

7. C
'Destructive' because it means causing harm or damage, which is the opposite of 'constructive.'

8. C
'To finish' because 'conclude' means to bring something to an end or reach a decision after considering facts or arguments.

9. C
'Crafty' because a crafty person is someone who is clever at achieving their aims through deceit or trickery.

10. D
'A sudden event causing widespread destruction' because a disaster refers to a catastrophic event that causes significant harm or damage.

11. A
'Entire' means whole or complete.

12. B
'Envy' is the correct answer as it refers to a feeling of discontented longing inspired by someone else's possessions.

13. C
'Fragile' describes something easily broken or damaged.

14. D
'Frequent' means happening often or at short intervals.

15. D
'Humble' is the correct answer as it means having or showing a modest or low estimate of one's importance.

16. B
'Impact' refers to a powerful effect or influence that something has on another.

17. C
'Mature' describes someone or something that is fully developed or grown.

18. C
'Mistrust' refers to having a lack of confidence in someone or something.

19. C
'Outstanding' means something that is remarkable, exceptional, or excellent.

20. D
'Peer' refers to someone who is of the same age group or social standing as oneself.

21. A
When you prefer something, it means you like it more than other options.

22. B
Feeling queasy refers to feeling sick or nauseated.

23. B
'Reduce' because reducing something means making it smaller in size, amount, or number.

24. A
Resist' because resisting means trying to stop or avoid something.

25. B
'Reveal' because revealing means making something known or visible that was hidden or secret.

26. B
'Shabby' describes something that is worn out and in poor condition.

27. A
'Sole' means being the only one; single or exclusive.

28. A
'Sturdy' describes something that is strong, well-built, and robust.

29. B
'Tradition' refers to customs, beliefs, or practices that are passed down through generations.

30. C
'Variety' refers to a collection of diverse or different things.

Verbal Battery - Sentence Completion

The CCAT Verbal Battery - Sentence Completion section is designed to evaluate your ability to understand and complete sentences based on context and word usage.

Example: She _____ to the store to buy groceries.

Objective: Evaluate vocabulary knowledge, contextual understanding, and the ability to integrate information to form coherent sentences.

Quiz 1 Answer Sheet

	A	B	C	D	E		A	B	C	D	E
1	○	○	○	○	○	21	○	○	○	○	○
2	○	○	○	○	○	22	○	○	○	○	○
3	○	○	○	○	○	23	○	○	○	○	○
4	○	○	○	○	○	24	○	○	○	○	○
5	○	○	○	○	○	25	○	○	○	○	○
6	○	○	○	○	○						
7	○	○	○	○	○						
8	○	○	○	○	○						
9	○	○	○	○	○						
10	○	○	○	○	○						
11	○	○	○	○	○						
12	○	○	○	○	○						
13	○	○	○	○	○						
14	○	○	○	○	○						
15	○	○	○	○	○						
16	○	○	○	○	○						
17	○	○	○	○	○						
18	○	○	○	○	○						
19	○	○	○	○	○						
20	○	○	○	○	○						

1. I _____ to the park every Sunday with my family.

    A. go   B. going
    C. goes   D. went

2. She couldn't _____ to buy the new toy.

    A. afford   B. conclude
    C. hardship D. permit

3. I _____ that the school will close early today.

    A. permit   B. conclude
    C. hardship D. surface

4. The family faced financial _____ after the breadwinner lost his job.

    A. surface   B. afford
    C. hardship   D. permit

5. Please _____ me to go out with my friends.

    A. surface   B. afford
    C. permit   D. conclude

6. A shiny object glinted on the _____ of the water.

    A. permit   B. conclude
    C. surface   D. afford

7. She _____ her homework before dinner.

    A. do   B. doing
    C. does   D. did

8. We _____ a movie last night.

    A. watching   B. watch
    C. watched   D. watches

9. They usually _____ soccer on Saturdays.

    A. play   B. playing
    C. plays   D. played

10. He _____ his lunch at school every day.

    A. ate   B. eat
    C. eating   D. eats

11. The cat _____ on the chair now.

    A. is sitting   B. sat
    C. sitting   D. sits

12. She _____ her homework every day.

    A. doing   B. does
    C. do   D. done

13. I _____ basketball with my friends after school everyday.

    A. play   B. playing
    C. plays   D. played

14. The birds _____ in the garden every morning.

    A. flies   B. flying
    C. fly   C. flown

15. He _____ his bicycle to school.

    A. ride   B. rode
    C. riding   D. rides

16. The explorer ventured into the _____ jungle, filled with exotic animals and plants.

    A. source   B. weary
    C. vast   D. proceed

17. Despite his success, John remained humble and lived a _____ life.

    A. source   B. modest
    C. vast   D. proceed

18. After a long day's work, Sarah felt _____ and just wanted to relax.

    A. source   B. weary
    C. vast   D. proceed

19. The meeting will _____ as planned, starting at 10 a.m. sharp.

    A. source   B. weary

    C. vast   D. proceed

20. He traced the river back to its _____, a small spring deep in the mountains.

    A. source   B. weary

    C. vast   D. proceed

ANSWER KEY

1. A
In the present tense, we use 'go' with 'I.'

2. A
Afford means to have enough money to purchase something.

3. B
Conclude means to come to a decision based on reasoning or evidence.

4. C
Hardship refers to difficult circumstances or adversity.

5. C
Permit means to allow or give consent for something.

6. C
Surface refers to the top layer of something.

7. C
In the present tense, 'does' is used with 'she.'

8. C
'Watched' is the past tense of 'watch.'

9. A
'Play' is used in the present tense with 'they.'

10. D
'Eats' is the correct form in the present tense with 'he.'

11. A
'Is sitting,' is used because the sentence includes 'now.'

12. B
This sentence requires the simple present tense 'does' to show a habitual action done regularly.

13. A
Here, the present simple tense 'play' is used to express a routine or habitual activity.

14. C
The present simple tense 'fly' is used to indicate a regular action done by the birds.

15. D
This sentence requires the simple present tense 'rides' to describe his routine action of using the bicycle for commuting.

16. C
'Vast' describes a jungle that is large and extensive.

17. B
'Modest' here means living a simple life despite success.

18. B
'Weary' means feeling tired or exhausted.

19. D
'Proceed' means to continue or go forward, often referring to a scheduled event.

20. A
'Source' means the origin or starting point of something, for example, a river.

Verbal Analogies

The Verbal Battery specifically measures a student's ability to understand and reason using concepts, assessing verbal reasoning, comprehension, and the capacity to use language in problem-solving tasks.

Components of the Verbal Battery

Verbal Analogies:

Description: Students are presented with pairs of words that share a relationship. They must identify a similar relationship between a new pair of words.

Example: Dog is to Puppy as Cat is to _____.

Objective: Assess the ability to discern relationships between words and apply logical reasoning to identify analogous pairs.

TIPS FOR ANSWERING

Read Carefully: Ensure you understand each word and the relationships presented. Misinterpretation can lead to incorrect answers.

Identify Relationships: Determine the relationship between the first pair of words before selecting the analogous pair.

Quiz 1 Answer Sheet

	A	B	C	D	E		A	B	C	D	E
1	○	○	○	○	○	21	○	○	○	○	○
2	○	○	○	○	○	22	○	○	○	○	○
3	○	○	○	○	○	23	○	○	○	○	○
4	○	○	○	○	○	24	○	○	○	○	○
5	○	○	○	○	○	25	○	○	○	○	○
6	○	○	○	○	○	26	○	○	○	○	○
7	○	○	○	○	○	27	○	○	○	○	○
8	○	○	○	○	○	28	○	○	○	○	○
9	○	○	○	○	○	29	○	○	○	○	○
10	○	○	○	○	○	30	○	○	○	○	○
11	○	○	○	○	○						
12	○	○	○	○	○						
13	○	○	○	○	○						
14	○	○	○	○	○						
15	○	○	○	○	○						
16	○	○	○	○	○						
17	○	○	○	○	○						
18	○	○	○	○	○						
19	○	○	○	○	○						
20	○	○	○	○	○						

Instructions: Choose the option with the same relationship.

1. Pork : Pig :: Beef :

a. Herd b. Farmer

c. Cow d. Lamb

2. Fruit : Banana :: Mammal :

a. Cow b. Snake

c. Fish d. Sparrow

3. Slumber : Sleep :: Bog :

a. Dream b. Foray

c. Swamp d. Night

4. Zoology : Animals

    a. Ecology : Pollution

    b. Botany : Plants

    c. Chemistry : Atoms

    d. History : People

5. Child : Human

    a. Dog : Pet

    b. Kitten : Cat

    c. Cow : Milk

    d. Bird : Robin

6. Wax : Candle

   a. Ink : Pen

   b. Clay : Bowl

   c. String : Kite

   d. Liquid : Cup

7. Which word does not belong with the others?

   a. Jet   b. Float Plane

   c. Kite   d. Biplane

8. Which of the following does not belong?

    a. Number   b. Denominate

    c. Numerate   d. Figure

9. Which of the following does not belong?

    a. Abc   b. bCD

    c. Nmo   d. Pqr

10. Which of the following does not belong?

    a. CD   b. OP

    c. LM   d. BD

11. Which of the following does not belong?

   a. 121212   b. 141414

   c. 151415   d. 292929

12. Which of the following does not belong?

   a. 246   b. 123

   c. 468   d. 24

13. Which of the following does not belong?

   a. aBCd   b. lMNo

   c. PQrs   d. tUVw

14. Which of the following does not belong?

    a. ABCD   b. JKLM

    c. PQRS   d. WXYZ

15. Which of the following does not belong?

    a. BBCCDDEE   b. LLMMNNOO

    c. HHIIJJKK   d. RRSSTTUU

16. Which of the following does not belong?

    a. def   b. nop

    c. tuv   d. lmn

17. Which of the following does not belong?

    a. Argue   b. Talk

    c. Dispute   d. Contest

18. Winner : Champion :: Sheen :

    a. Shimmer   b. Dark

    c. Sweet   d. Garbage

19. Frog : Amphibian :: Snake :

    a. Reptile   b. Bacteria

    c. Protozoan   d. Mammal

20. Petal : Flower :: Fur

    a. Coat   b. Warm

    c. Woman   d. Rabbit

21. Present : Birthday :: Reward :

    a. Accomplishment   b. Medal

    c. Acceptance   d. Cash

22. Shovel : Dig :: Scissors :

    a. Scoop   b. Carry

    c. Snip   d. Rip

23. Finger : Hand :: Leg :

    a. Body   b. Foot

    c. Toe   d. Hip

24. Sleep in : Late :: Skip breakfast :

    a. Hungry   b. Early

    c. Lunch   d. Dinner

25. Circle : Sphere :: Square :

    a. Triangle   b. Oval

    c. Half Circle   d. Cube

26. Orange : Fruit :: Carrot:

    a. Vegetable   b. Bean

    c. Food   d. Apple

27. Which of the following does not belong?

    a. ddeeffgg   b. fgghhii

    c. nnooppqq   d. ttuuvvww

28. Which of the following does not belong?

    a. 11223344   b. 33445566

    c. 33455666   d. 44556677

29. Which of the following does not belong?

    a. mNo   b. pQr

    c. Stu   d. xYz

30. Which of the following does not belong?

a. abcabc

b. defdef

c. ghihij

d. mnomno

Answer Key

1. C
2. A
3. C
4. B
5. B
6. B
7. C
8. D
9. B
10. D
11. C
12. B
13. C
14. B
15. C
16. D
17. B
18. A
19. A
20. D
21. A
22. C
23. A
24. A
25. D
26. A
27. B
28. C
29. C
30. C

Quiz 2 Answer Sheet

	A	B	C	D	E		A	B	C	D	E
1	○	○	○	○	○	21	○	○	○	○	○
2	○	○	○	○	○	22	○	○	○	○	○
3	○	○	○	○	○	23	○	○	○	○	○
4	○	○	○	○	○	24	○	○	○	○	○
5	○	○	○	○	○	25	○	○	○	○	○
6	○	○	○	○	○	26	○	○	○	○	○
7	○	○	○	○	○	27	○	○	○	○	○
8	○	○	○	○	○	28	○	○	○	○	○
9	○	○	○	○	○	29	○	○	○	○	○
10	○	○	○	○	○	30	○	○	○	○	○
11	○	○	○	○							
12	○	○	○	○							
13	○	○	○	○							
14	○	○	○	○							
15	○	○	○	○							
16	○	○	○	○							
17	○	○	○	○							
18	○	○	○	○							
19	○	○	○	○							
20	○	○	○	○							

1. Which of the following does not belong?

    a. Dog   b. Wolf

    c. Terrier   d. Cougar

2. Which of the following does not belong?

    a. DDDdddEEE   b. MMMoooPPP

    c. GGGhhhIII   d. JJJkkkLLL

3. Which of the following does not belong?

    a. cde   b. mno

    c. stu   d. abc

4. Which of the following does not belong?

    a. 446688   b. 224466

    c. 336699   d. 66881010

5. Which of the following does not belong?

    a. Assume   b. Certain

    c. Sure   d. Positive

6. Which of the following does not belong?

    a. MnOp   b. AbCD

    c. QrSt   d. WxYz

7. Which of the following does not belong?

    a. Look   b. See

    c. Perceive   d. Surmise

8. Which of the following does not belong?

    a. Count   b. Number

    c. Add up   d. List

9. Which of the following does not belong?

    a. Secure   b. Discard

    c. Throw out   d. Abandon

10. PETAL is to FLOWER as FUR is to

a. Coat   b. Warm

c. Woman   d. Rabbit

11. PRESENT is to BIRTHDAY as REWARD is to

a. Accomplishment   b. Medal

c. Acceptance   d. Cash

12. SHOVEL is to DIG as SCISSORS is to

a. Scoop   b. Carry

c. Snip   d. Rip

13. FINGER is to HAND as LEG is to

    a. Body   b. Foot

    c. Toe   d. Hip

14. SLEEP IN is to LATE as SKIP BREAKFAST is

    a. Hungry   b. Early

    c. Lunch   d. Dinner

15. CIRCLE is to SPHERE as SQUARE is to   Triangle

    a. Oval   b. Half

    c. Circle   d. Cube

16. ORANGE is to FRUIT as CARROT is to

    a. Vegetable   b. Bean

    c. Food   d. Apple

17. PAPER is to LIGHT as LEAD is to

    a. Grey   b. Solid

    c. Thick   d. Heavy

18. STEEL is to CAR as GLASS is to

    a. Pane   b. Window

    c. Transparent   d. Fragile

19. FOUR-LEAF CLOVER is to LUCK as CROSS is to

   a. Christianity   b. Religion

   c. Wood   d. Tree

20. NEST is to BIRD as CAVE is to

   a. Bear   b. Petal

   c. House   d. Dog

21. TEACHER is to SCHOOL as WAITRESS is to

   a. Office   b. Coffee shop

   c. Customer   d. Student

22. PEBBLE is to BOULDER as POND is to

    a. Ocean   b. River

    c. Drop   d. Rapids

23. DOG is to POODLE as SHARK is to

    a. Great White   b. Dolphin

    c. Whale   d. Fish

24. FOX is to CHICKEN as CAT is to

    a. Rabbit   b. Mouse

    c. Cat   d. Hen

25. LAWYER is to TRIAL as DOCTOR is to

    a. Patient   b. Business man

    c. Operation   d. Nurse

26. EAT is to FAT as BREATHE is to

    a. Inhale   b. Live

    c. Drink   d. Talk

27. MELT is to LIQUID as FREEZE is to

    a. Ice   b. Condense

    c. Solid   d. Stream

28. CLOCK is to TIME as THERMOMETER is to

    a. Heat   b. Radiation

    c. Energy   d. Temperature

29. CAR is to GARAGE as PLANE is to

    a. Depot   b. Port

    c. Hanger   d. Harbour

30. ACTING is to THEATER as GAMBLING is to

    a. Gym   b. Bar

    c. Club   d. Casino

Answer Key

1. D
2. B
3. D
4. C
5. A
6. B
7. D
8. D
9. A
10. D
11. A
12. C
13. A
14. A
15. D
16. A
17. D
18. B
19. A
20. A
21. B
22. A
23. A
24. B
25. C
26. B
27. C
28. D
29. C
30. D

Non Verbal Battery

The Non-Verbal Battery evaluates reasoning and problem-solving skills through geometric shapes and figures, independent of language abilities.

Description: In this section, students are presented with sets of geometric figures that share a common attribute. The task is to identify the characteristic linking the given figures and select the option that best fits the same category.

Objective: Assess the ability to recognize patterns, categorize visual information, and apply logical reasoning without relying on verbal cues.

CLASSIFICATION

Instructions and Tips for Answering Figure Classification Questions:

Observe Common Features:

Examine the given figures to identify shared attributes, such as shape, size, color, shading, or patterns.

Analyze Answer Options:

Compare each choice against the identified common feature to determine which one aligns with the given set.

Eliminate Irrelevant Choices:

Cross out and eliminate options that do not share the common feature, narrowing down potential correct answers.

Consider Multiple Attributes:

Some questions may involve more than one common feature. Ensure all identified attributes are considered when selecting the answer.

Practice Visualizing:
Practice visualizing geometric figures and patterns to become familiar with different classifications.

Answer Sheet

	A	B	C	D
1	○	○	○	○
2	○	○	○	○
3	○	○	○	○
4	○	○	○	○
5	○	○	○	○
6	○	○	○	○
7	○	○	○	○
8	○	○	○	○
9	○	○	○	○
10	○	○	○	○
11	○	○	○	○
12	○	○	○	○
13	○	○	○	○
14	○	○	○	○
15	○	○	○	○
16	○	○	○	○
17	○	○	○	○
18	○	○	○	○
19	○	○	○	○
20	○	○	○	○

1. Select the choice that does not belong.

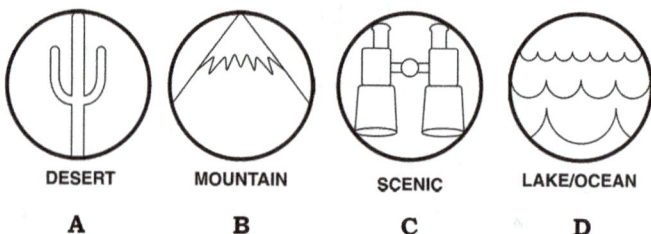

| DESERT | MOUNTAIN | SCENIC | LAKE/OCEAN |
| A | B | C | D |

2. Select the choice that does not belong.

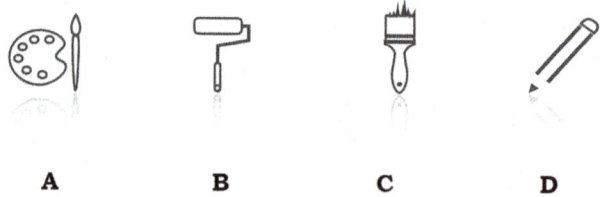

| A | B | C | D |

3. Select the choice that does not belong.

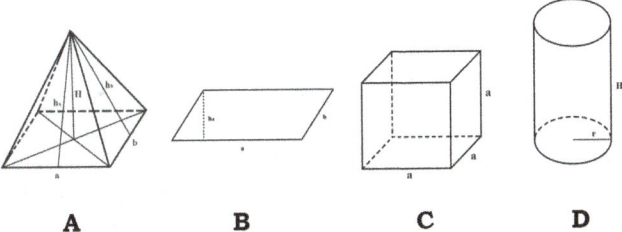

| A | B | C | D |

4. Select the choice that does not belong.

AB MN PR XY
   A   B   C   D

5. Select the choice that does not belong.

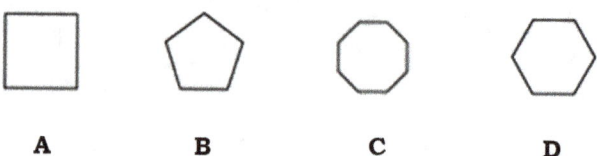

6. Select the choice that does not belong.

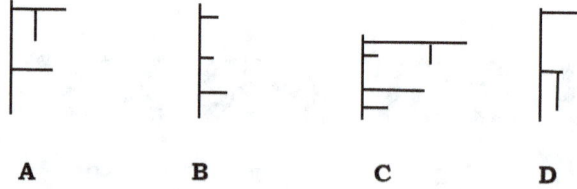

7. Select the choice that does not belong.

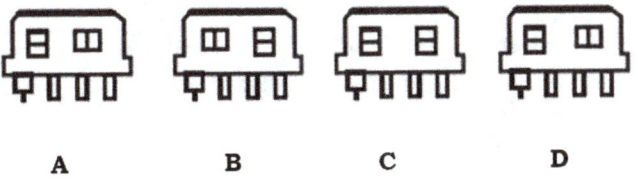

7	13	17	14
A	B	C	D

8. Select the choice that does not belong.

A B C D

9. Select the choice that does not belong.

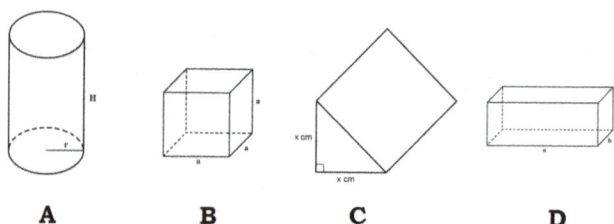

10. Select the choice that does not belong.

11. Select the choice that does not belong.

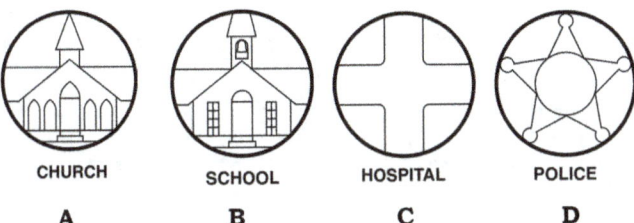

12. Select the choice that does not belong.

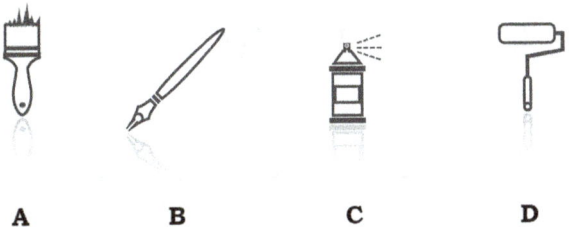

13. Select the choice that does not belong.

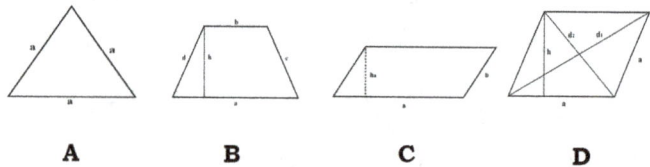

A   B   C   D

14. Select the choice that does not belong.

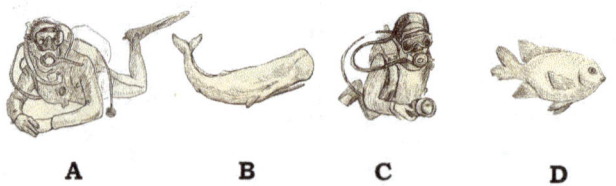

A   B   C   D

15. Select the choice that does not belong.

25   68   85   40
  A   B   C   D

16. Select the choice that does not belong.

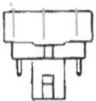

  A   B   C   D

17. Select the choice that does not belong.

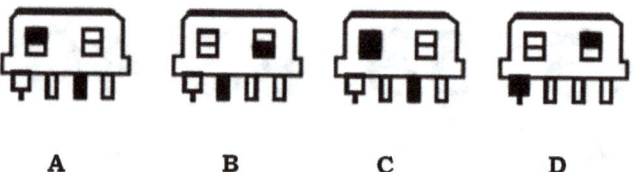

A B C D

18. Select the choice that does not belong.

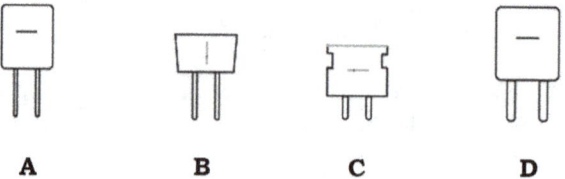

A B C D

19. Select the choice that does not belong.

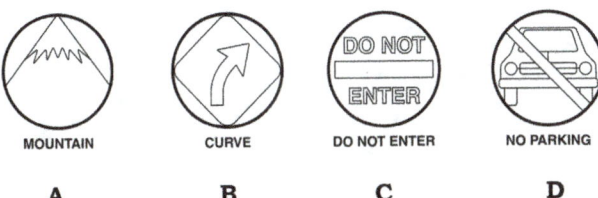

20. Select the choice that does not belong.

Answer Key

1. C
2. D
3. B
4. C
5. B
6. C
7. D
8. C
9. A
10. A
11. D
12. B
13. A
14. D
15. B
16. D
17. D
18. B
19. A
20. A

Verbal Battery - Classification Quiz 2

Answer Sheet

	A	B	C	D	E			A	B	C	D	E
1	○	○	○	○	○		21	○	○	○	○	○
2	○	○	○	○	○		22	○	○	○	○	○
3	○	○	○	○	○		23	○	○	○	○	○
4	○	○	○	○	○		24	○	○	○	○	○
5	○	○	○	○	○		25	○	○	○	○	○
6	○	○	○	○	○		26	○	○	○	○	○
7	○	○	○	○	○		27	○	○	○	○	○
8	○	○	○	○	○		28	○	○	○	○	○
9	○	○	○	○	○		29	○	○	○	○	○
10	○	○	○	○	○		30	○	○	○	○	○
11	○	○	○	○	○							
12	○	○	○	○	○							
13	○	○	○	○	○							
14	○	○	○	○	○							
15	○	○	○	○	○							
16	○	○	○	○	○							
17	○	○	○	○	○							
18	○	○	○	○	○							
19	○	○	○	○	○							
20	○	○	○	○	○							

Analogies

1. Which of the following does not belong?

    a. Dog   b. Wolf

    c. Terrier   `d. Cougar

2. Which of the following does not belong?

    a. DDDdddEEE   b. MMMoooPPP

    c. GGGhhhIII   d. JJJkkkLLL

3. Which of the following does not belong?

    a. cde   b. mno

    c. stu   d. abc

4. Which of the following does not belong?

    a. 446688   b. 224466
    c. 336699   d. 66881010

5. Which of the following does not belong?

    a. Assume   b. Certain
    c. Sure   d. Positive

6. Which of the following does not belong?

    a. MnOp   b. AbCD
    c. QrSt   d. WxYz

7. Which of the following does not belong?

    a. Look   b. See
    c. Perceive   d. Surmise

8. Which of the following does not belong?

    a. Count   b. Number
    c. Add up   d. List

9. Which of the following does not belong?

    a. Secure   b. Discard
    c. Throw out   d. Abandon

10. PETAL is to FLOWER as FUR is to

   a. Coat   b. Warm
   c. Woman   d. Rabbit

11. PRESENT is to BIRTHDAY as REWARD is to

   a. Accomplishment   b. Medal
   c. Acceptance   d. Cash

12. SHOVEL is to DIG as SCISSORS is to

   a. Scoop   b. Carry
   c. Snip   d. Rip

13. FINGER is to HAND as LEG is to

   a. Body   b. Foot
   c. Toe   d. Hip

14. SLEEP IN is to LATE as SKIP BREAKFAST is

    a. Hungy   b. Early
    c. Lunch   d. Dinner

15. CIRCLE is to SPHERE as SQUARE is to

    a. Triangle   b. Oval
    c. Half Circle d. Cube

16. ORANGE is to FRUIT as CARROT is to

    a. Vegetable   b. Bean
    c. Food   d. Apple

17. PAPER is to LIGHT as LEAD is to

    a. Grey   b. Solid
    c. Thick   d. Heavy

18. STEEL is to CAR as GLASS is to

    a. Pane   b. Window
    c. Transparent   d. Fragile

19. FOUR-LEAF CLOVER is to LUCK as CROSS is to

    a. Christianity   b. Religion
    c. Wood   d. Tree

20. NEST is to BIRD as CAVE is to

    a. Bear   b. Petal
    c. House   d. Dog

21. TEACHER is to SCHOOL as WAITRESS is to

    a. Office   b. Coffee shop
    c. Customer   d. Student

Analogies

22. PEBBLE is to BOULDER as POND is to

    a. Ocean   b. River
    c. Drop   d. Rapids

23. DOG is to POODLE as SHARK is to

    a. Great White   b. Dolphin
    c. Whale   d. Fish

24. FOX is to CHICKEN as CAT is to

    a. Rabbit   b. Mouse
    c. Cat   d. Hen

25. LAWYER is to TRIAL as DOCTOR is to

    a. Patient   b. Business man
    c. Operation   d. Nurse

26. EAT is to FAT as BREATHE is to

   a. Inhale   b. Live
   c. Drink   d. Talk

27. MELT is to LIQUID as FREEZE is to

   a. Ice   b. Condense
   c. Solid   d. Stream

28. CLOCK is to TIME as THERMOMETER is to

   a. Heat   b. Radiation
   c. Energy d. Temperature

29. CAR is to GARAGE as PLANE is to

   a. Depot   b. Port
   c. Hanger d. Harbour

30. ACTING is to THEATER as GAMBLING is to

a. Gym
b. Bar
c. Club
d. Casino

Answer Key

1. D
2. B
3. D
4. C
5. A
6. B
7. D
8. D
9. A
10. D
11. A
12. C
13. A
14. A
15. D
16. A
17. D
18. B
19. A
20. A
21. B
22. A
23. A
24. B
25. C
26. B
27. C
28. D
29. C
30. D

NON VERBAL BATTERY - FOLDING

The folding questions of the Non-Verbal Battery, you are shown a series of images that represent how a piece of paper is unfolded. Your task is to determine what the paper will look when it is folded.

Folding questions often test your spatial reasoning skills by asking you to visualize how a two-dimensional shape folds into a three-dimensional object. These questions can appear challenging, but with a clear strategy, you can approach them confidently. Follow these steps:

1. Understand the Question
Carefully read the instructions and review the shape presented and the choices.

Identify the folds or lines on the two-dimensional diagram. These lines indicate where the paper will be folded.

2. Visualize the Fold
Imagine folding the shape along the lines step by step.
Pay attention to how each section aligns with the section next to it after folding.

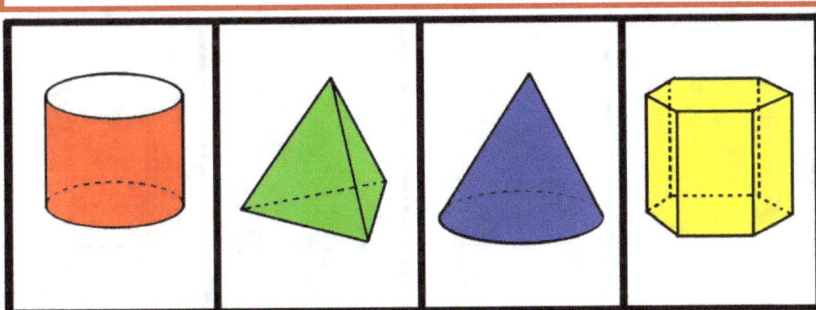

3. Look for Clues

- **Matching Edges:** Check for patterns, symbols, or colors that should align when folded.

- **Shaded or Marked Areas:** Notice shaded or marked areas that provide hints about the resulting shape.

- **Position of Tabs or Flaps:** Consider which sections will become edges, faces, or corners.

Use your fingers to "trace" folds mentally, imagining how the shape will form.

4. Eliminate Wrong Answers
This is the best strategy for any multiple choice question. Compare the given answer choices to your visualization. Eliminate the most obviously incorrect answers.

Focus on details like symmetry, alignment, and matching edges to narrow down your choices.

Discard options that:

- Mis-align patterns or symbols.

- Have the wrong shape or dimensions.

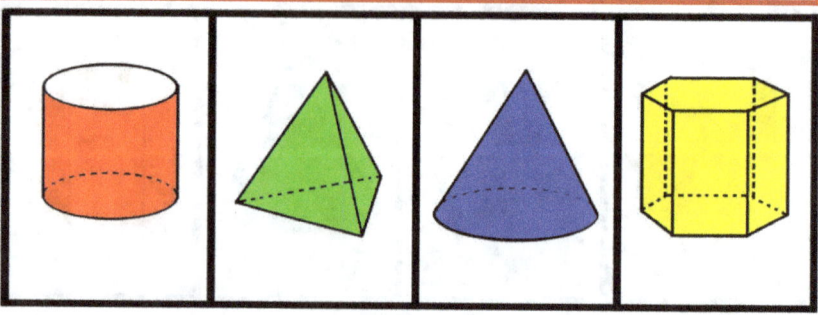

- Show impossible configurations (e.g., overlapping faces or incorrect angles).

6. Sketch if Allowed
If the test permits scratch paper, sketch the folds to better visualize the 3D object.

Mark which parts of the flat diagram correspond to specific sides of the folded shape.

7. Double-Check Your Choice
Revisit the question and ensure your answer matches the expected folded shape. Good advice for any type of question on a test.

Confirm the chosen option aligns with all visible folds, patterns, and angles.

Folding Answer Sheet - Quiz 1

	A	B	C	D
1	○	○	○	○
2	○	○	○	○
3	○	○	○	○
4	○	○	○	○
5	○	○	○	○
6	○	○	○	○
7	○	○	○	○
8	○	○	○	○
9	○	○	○	○
10	○	○	○	○
11	○	○	○	○
12	○	○	○	○
13	○	○	○	○
14	○	○	○	○
15	○	○	○	○
16	○	○	○	○
17	○	○	○	○
18	○	○	○	○
19	○	○	○	○
20	○	○	○	○

1. When the two longest sides touch what will the shape be?

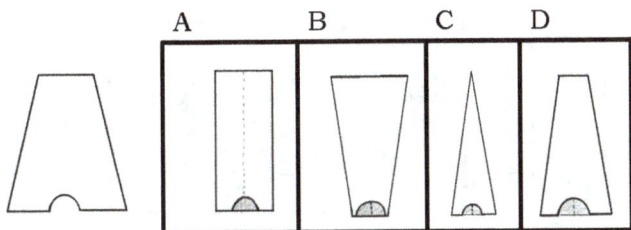

2. When folded, what pattern is possible?

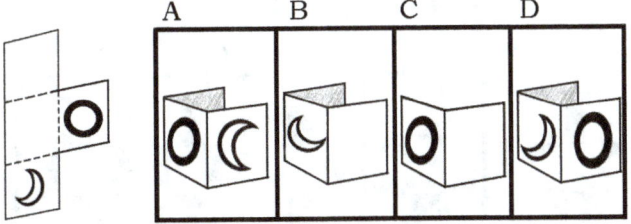

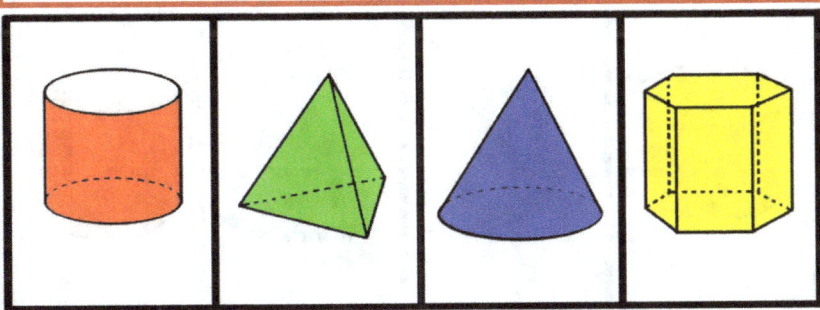

3. When folded into a loop, what will the strip of paper look like?

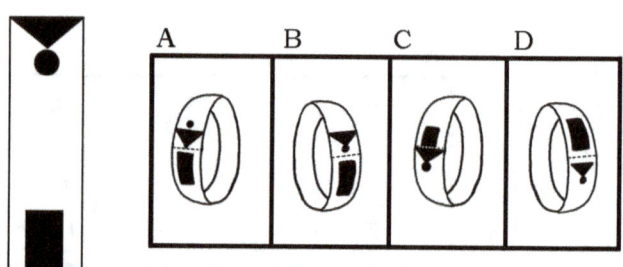

4. Which of the choices is the same pattern at a different angle?

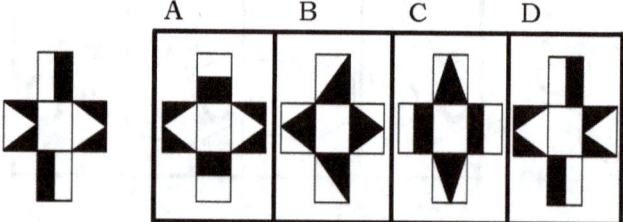

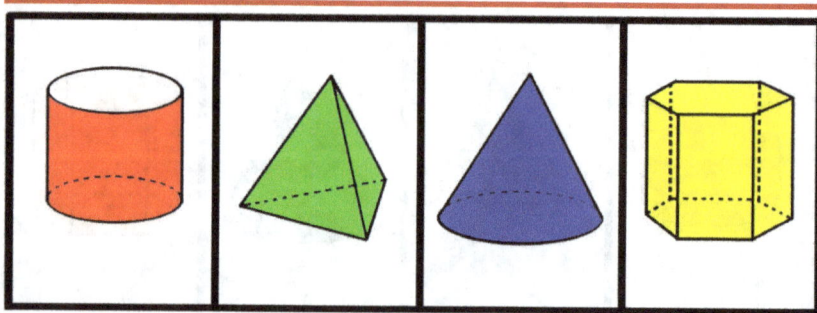

5. When put together, what 3-dimensional shape will you get?

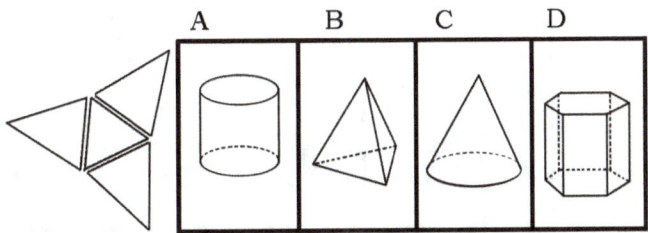

6. When folded, what pattern is possible?

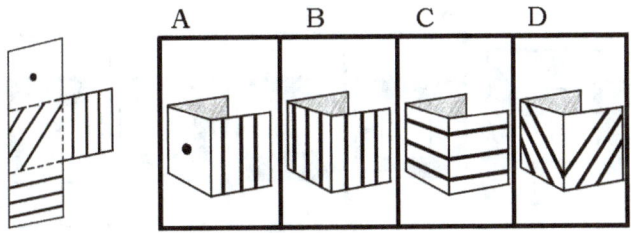

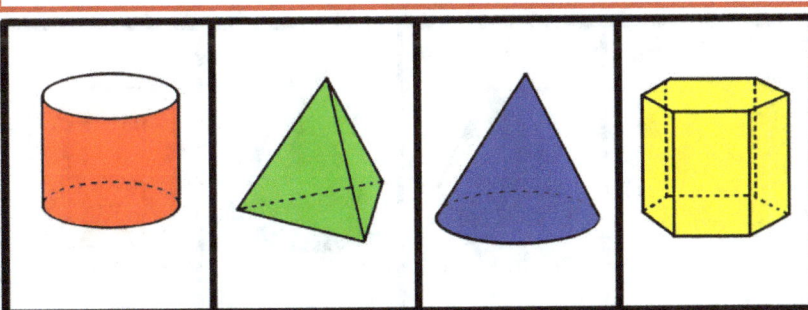

7. When folded into a loop, what will the strip of paper look like?

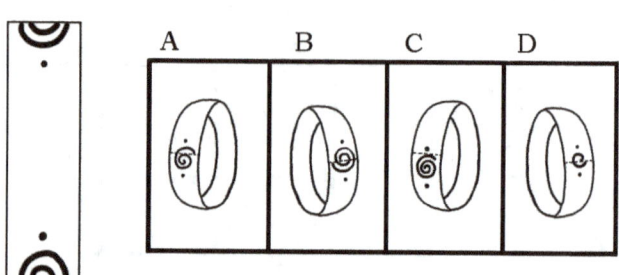

8. Which of the choices is the same pattern at a different angle?

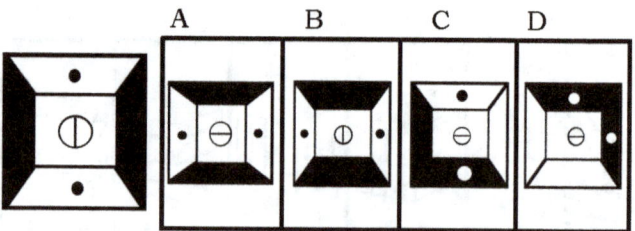

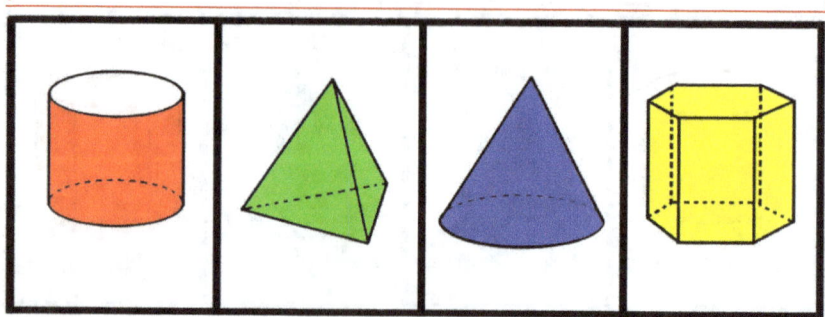

9. When folded, which shape will you get?

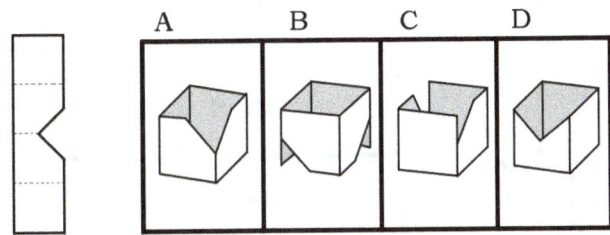

10. When folded, what pattern is possible?

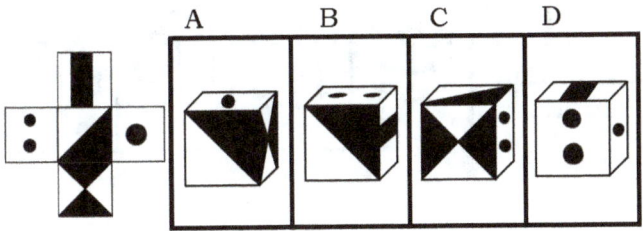

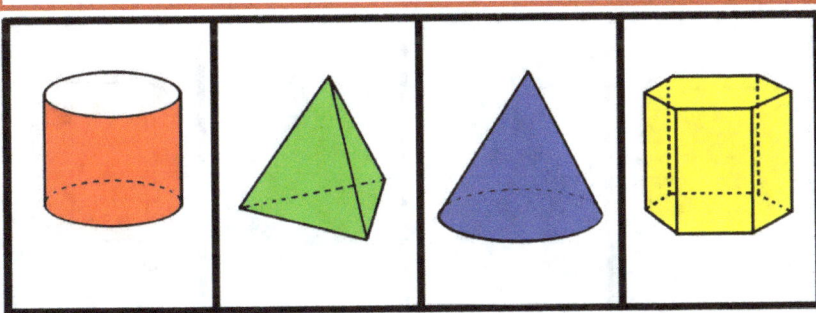

11. When folded, which shape is possible?

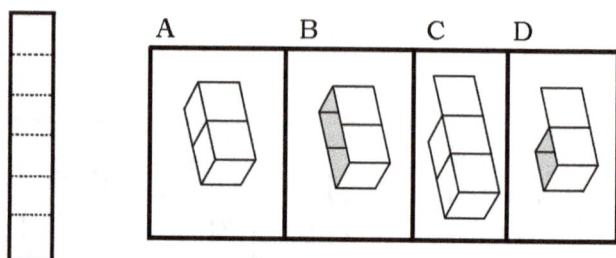

12. When folded, what pattern is possible?

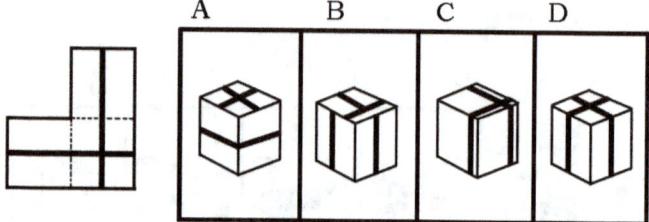

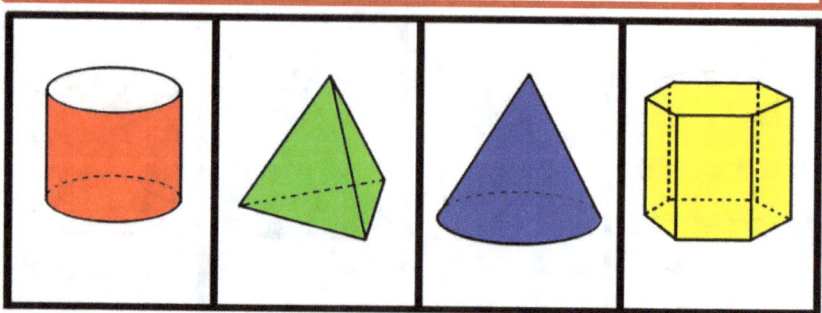

13. When folded into a loop, what will the strip of paper look like?

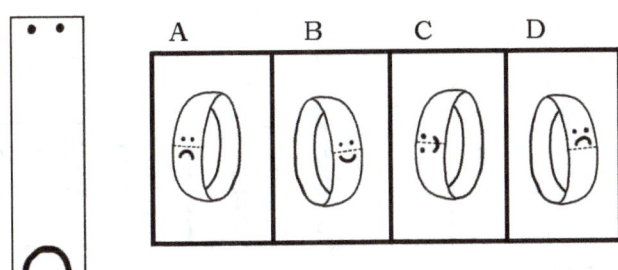

14. Which of the choices is the same pattern at a different angle?

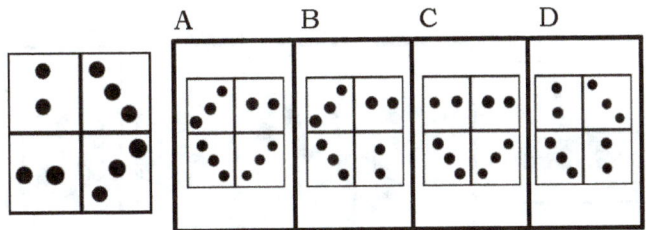

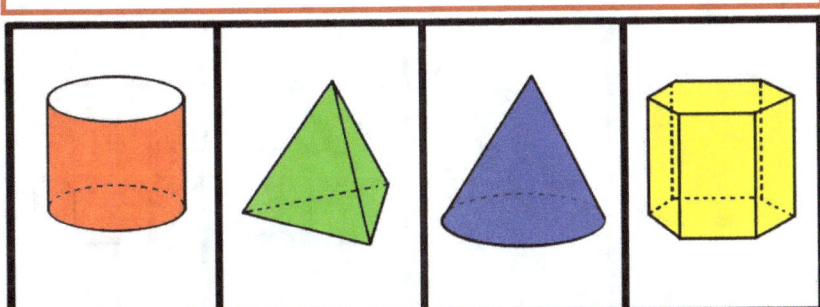

15. When folded along the dotted lines, which shape will you get?

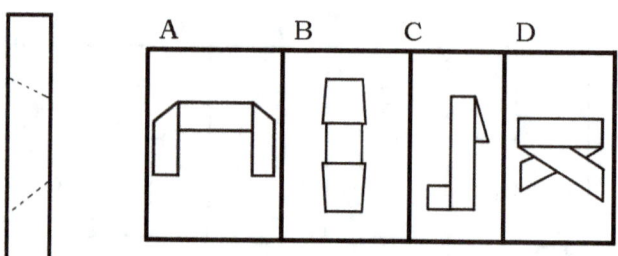

16. When folded, what pattern is possible?

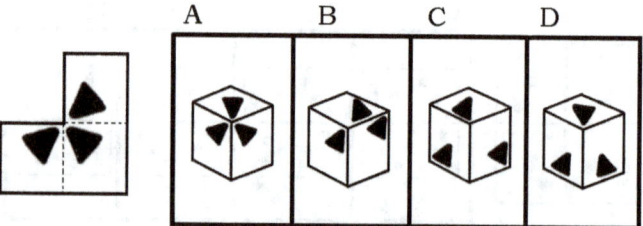

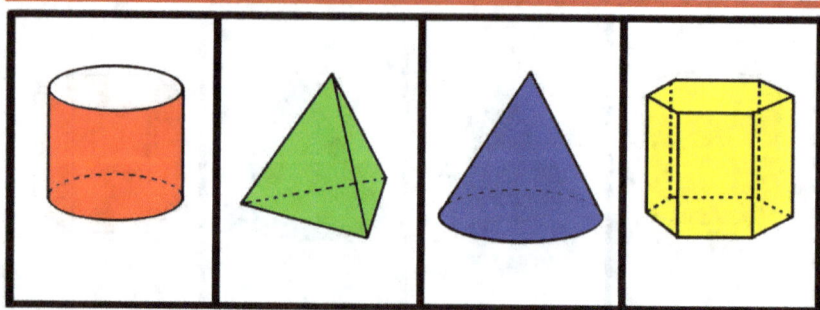

17. When folded into a loop, what will the strip of paper look like?

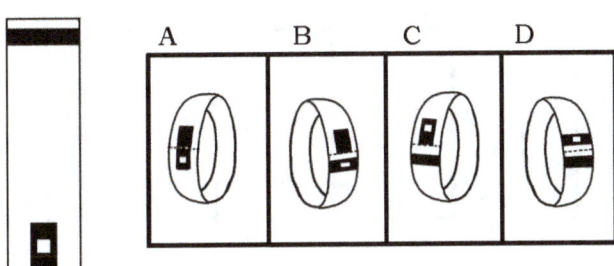

18. Which of the choices is the same pattern at a different angle?

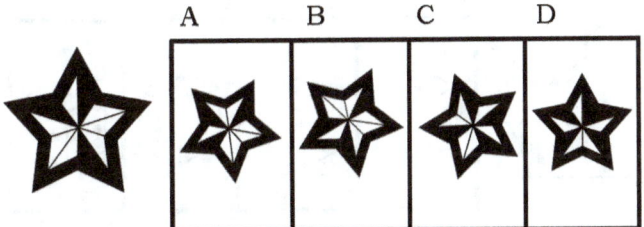

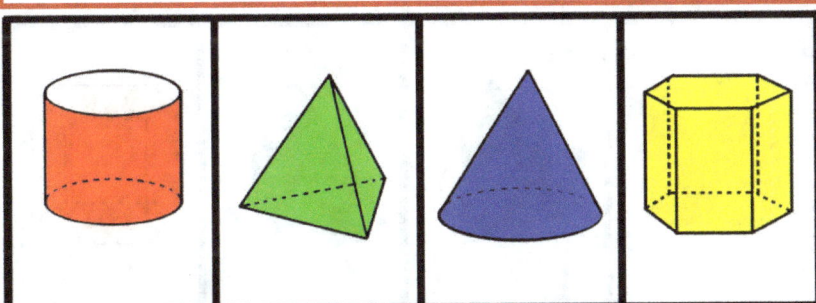

19. When folded along the dotted line, which shape will you get?

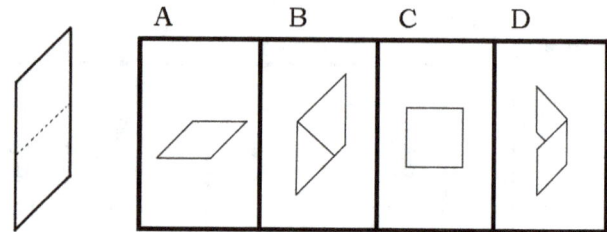

20. When folded, what pattern is possible?

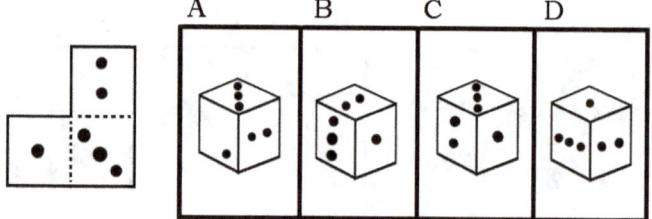

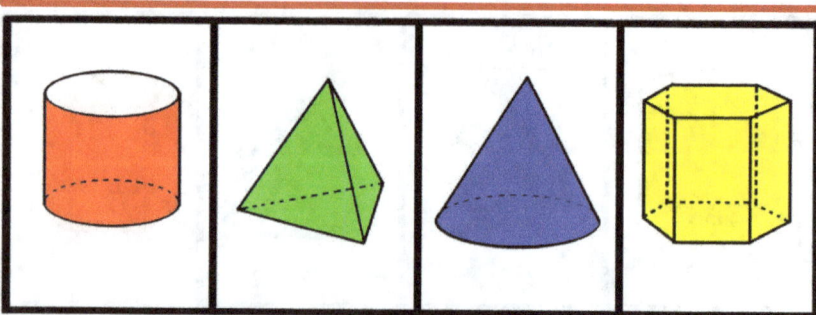

Answer Key

1. D
2. A
3. C
4. B
5. B
6. C
7. B
8. A
9. A
10. A
11. B
12. D
13. B
14. B
15. A
16. A
17. C
18. B
19. D
20. C

Folding Quiz 2 Answer Sheet

	A	B	C	D
1	○	○	○	○
2	○	○	○	○
3	○	○	○	○
4	○	○	○	○
5	○	○	○	○
6	○	○	○	○
7	○	○	○	○
8	○	○	○	○
9	○	○	○	○
10	○	○	○	○
11	○	○	○	○
12	○	○	○	○
13	○	○	○	○
14	○	○	○	○
15	○	○	○	○
16	○	○	○	○
17	○	○	○	○
18	○	○	○	○
19	○	○	○	○
20	○	○	○	○

1. When folded along the dotted lines, which shape will you get?

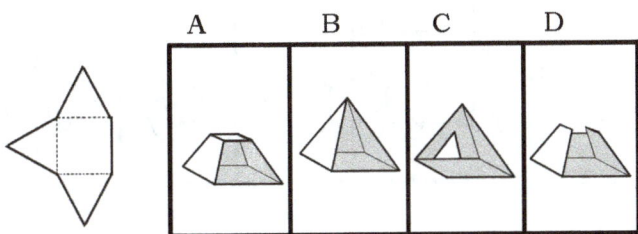

2. When folded, what pattern is possible?

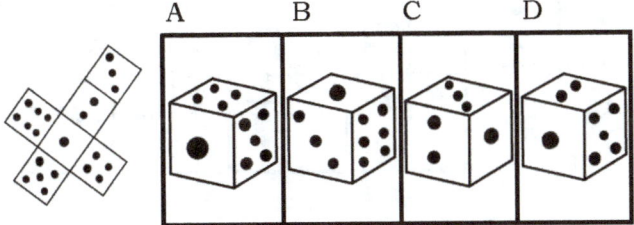

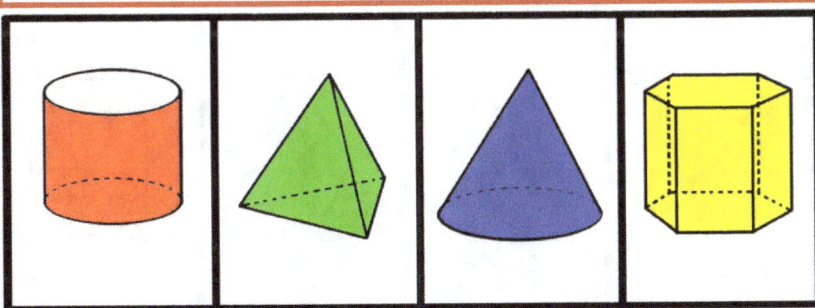

3. When folded into a loop, what will the strip of paper look like?

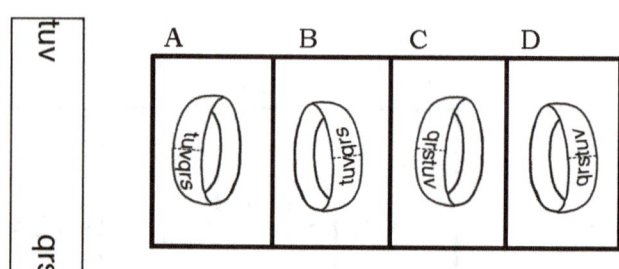

4. Which of the choices is the same pattern at a different angle?

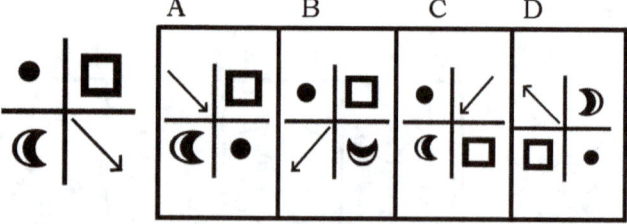

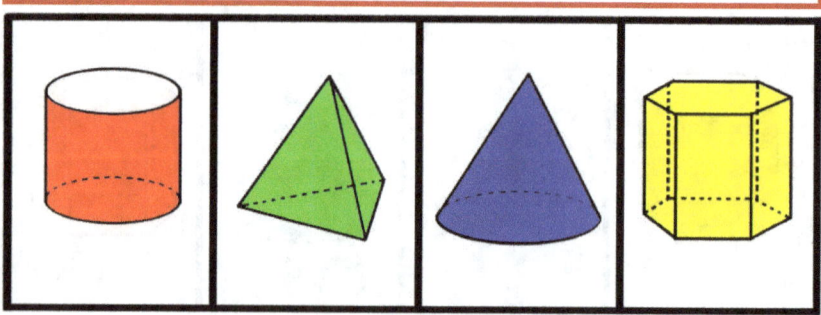

5. When put together, what 3-dimensional shape will you get?

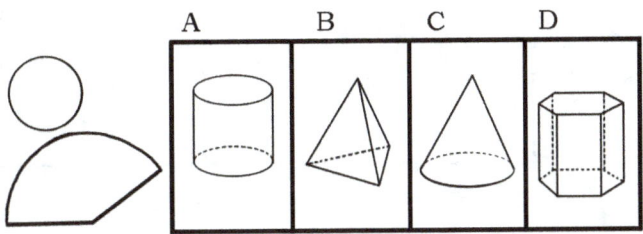

6. When folded, what pattern is possible?

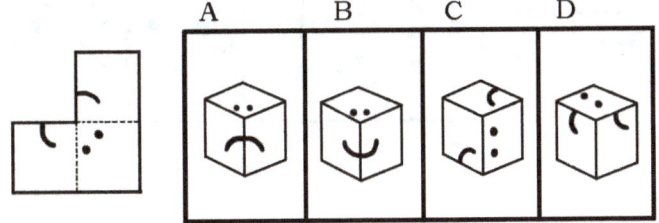

7. When folded, what pattern is possible?

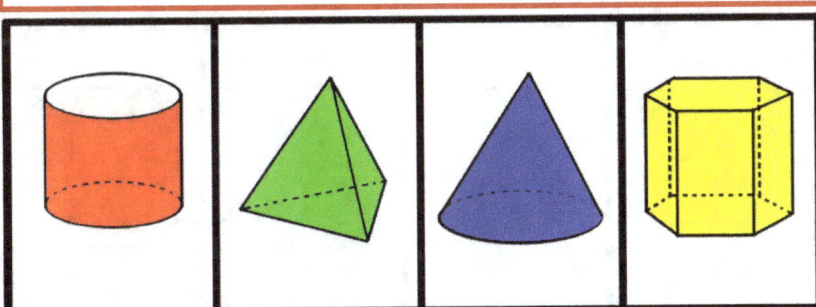

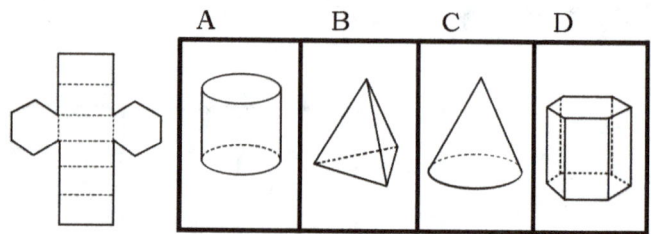

8. Which of the choices is the same pattern at a different angle?

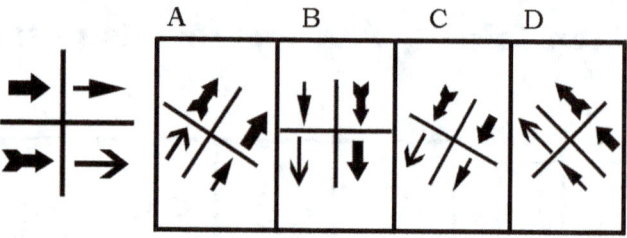

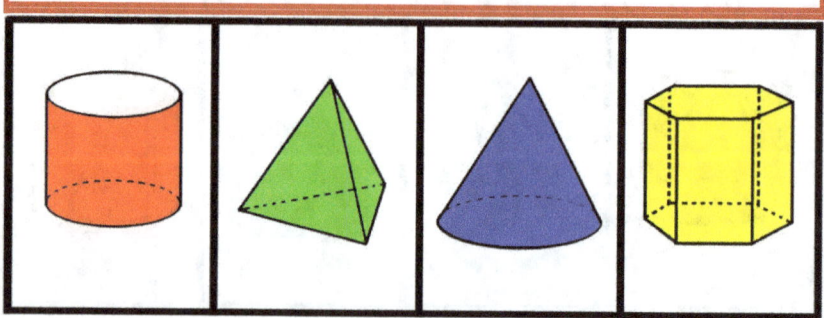

9. When put together, what 3-dimensional shape will you get?

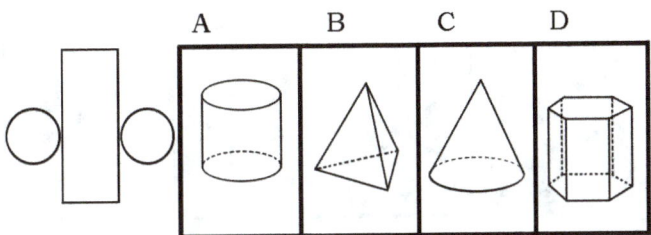

10. When folded into a loop, what will the strip of paper look like?

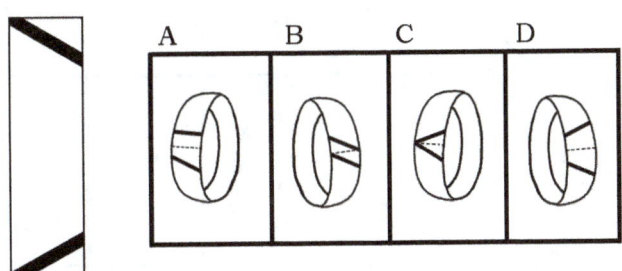

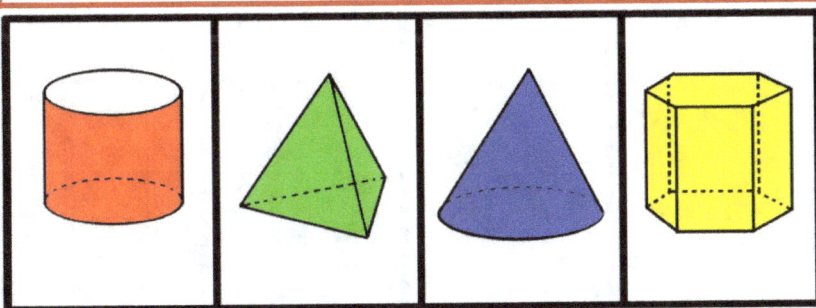

11. Which of the choices is the same pattern at a different angle?

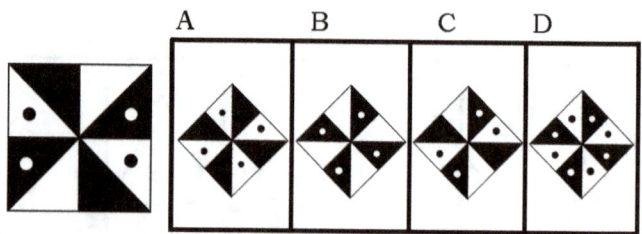

12. When put together, what 3-dimensional shape will you get?

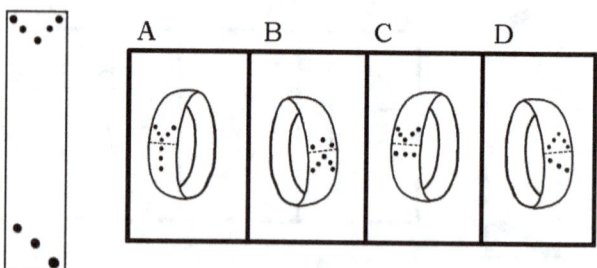

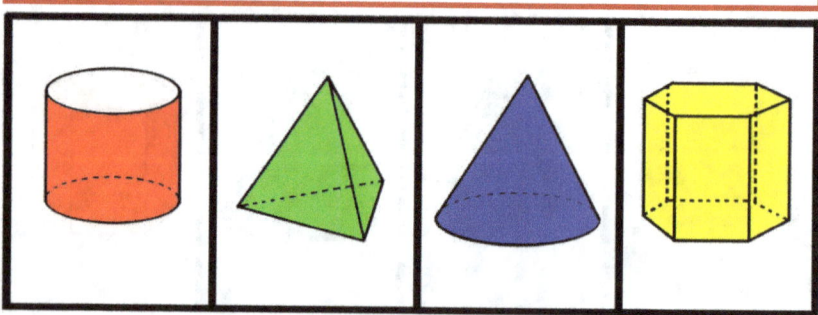

13. When folded into a loop, what will the strip of paper look like?

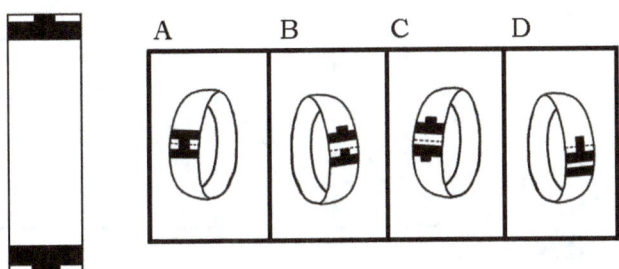

14. Which of the choices is the same pattern at a different angle?

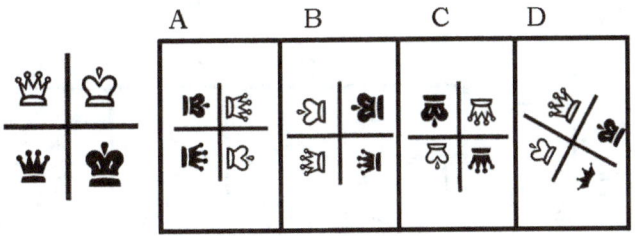

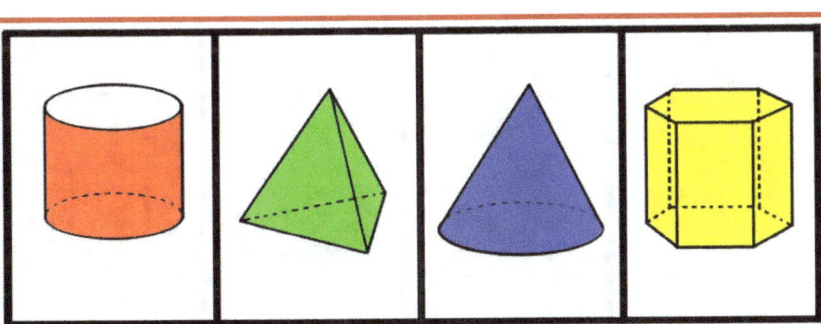

15. When folded into a loop, what will the strip of paper look like?

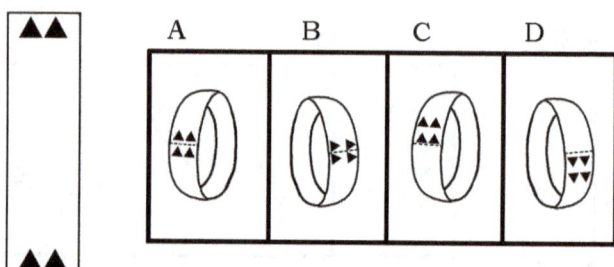

16. When folded, what pattern is possible?

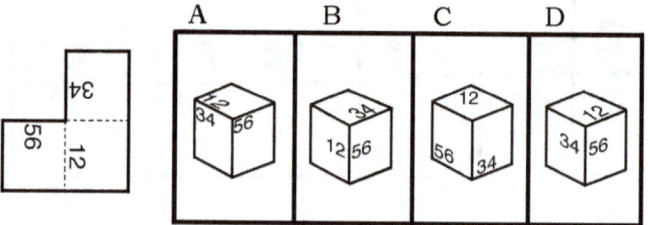

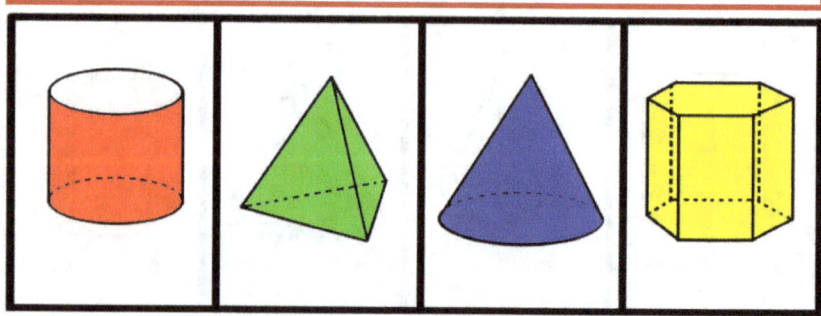

Folding

17. When folded into a loop, what will the strip of paper look like?

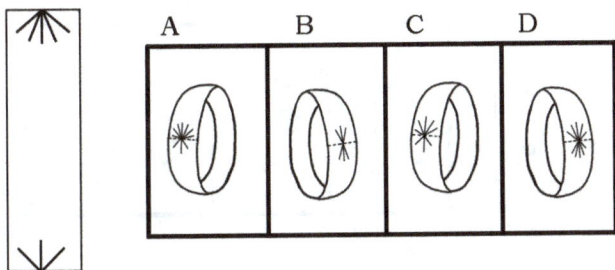

18. Which of the choices is the same pattern at a different angle?

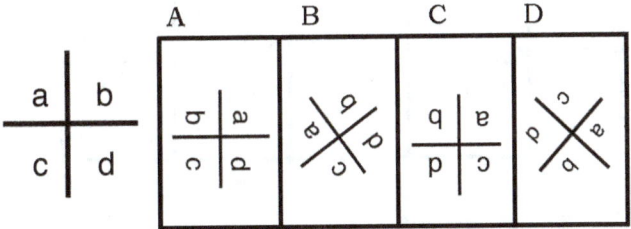

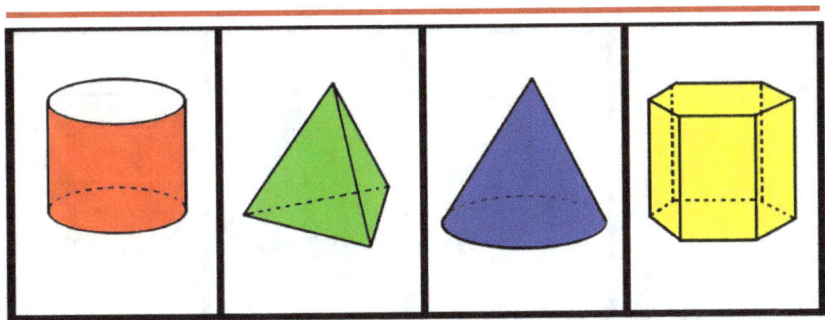

19. When folded, what pattern is possible?

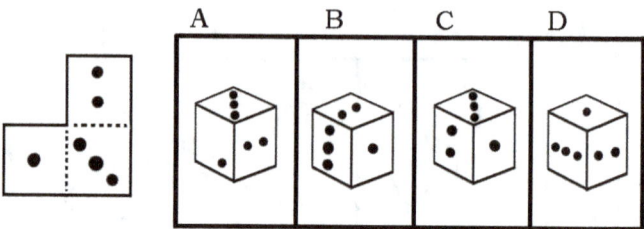

20. Which of the choices is the same pattern at a different angle?

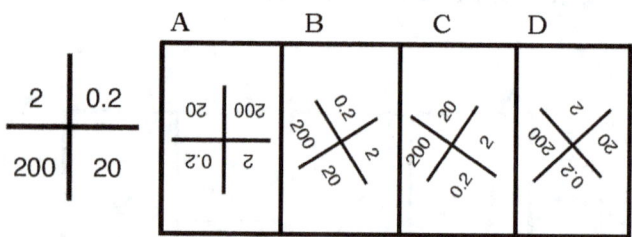

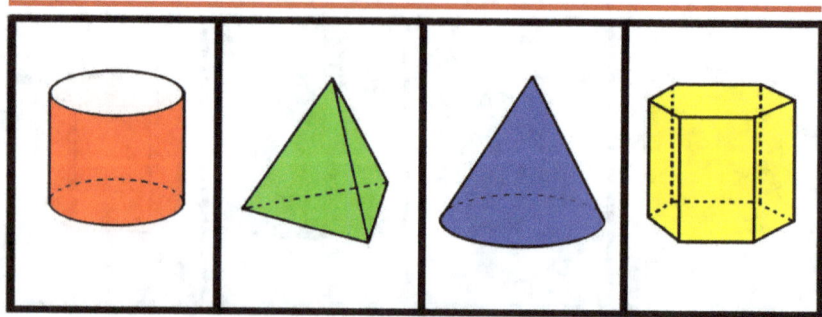

ANSWER KEY

1. B
2. A
3. D
4. D
5. C
6. B
7. D
8. C
9. A
10. C
11. C

12. D
13. A
14. B
15. A
16. D
17. C
18. D
19. C
20. A

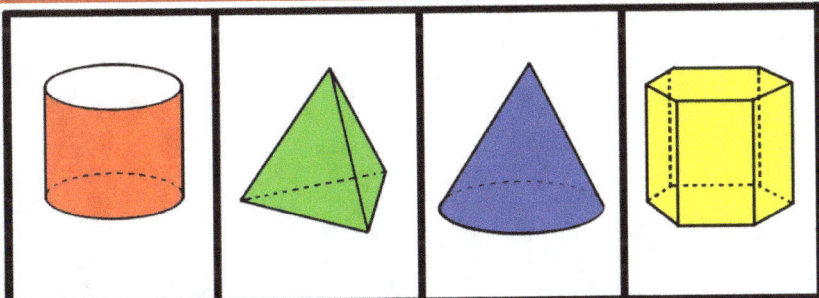

Non Verbal - Figure Matrix

Figure Matrices questions involve patterns of shapes, lines, or symbols arranged in a grid. The grid has two or three rows and tow or three columns, with one of the spaces empty. The task is to figure out the pattern or relationship between the shapes in the rows or columns and choose the correct answer to complete the grid.

These questions test your ability to spot patterns, understand how shapes change, and think logically. For example, shapes might get bigger, rotate, change colors, or follow a sequence as you move across the grid.

Instructions

Look at the Rows and Columns Carefully

Each row or column follows a specific rule or pattern. Start by looking at how the shapes, sizes, colors, or positions change from one box to the next.

Find the Pattern

Ask yourself

- Do the shapes change size or rotate?

- Is there a sequence in colors or the number of shapes?

- Are shapes being added or removed?

Look for rules that are the same across the rows.

Focus on the Missing Spot

Once you understand the pattern, think about what the missing box should look like. Use the rules you discovered to figure out the answer.

Check the Choices

Look at the answer choices provided. Compare them to the pattern and eliminate the ones that don't match.

Take Your Time and Double-Check

If you're not sure, review the pattern again to see if you missed anything. Sometimes, the answer becomes clearer when you look at the problem a second time.

Answer Sheet

	A	B	C	D
1	○	○	○	○
2	○	○	○	○
3	○	○	○	○
4	○	○	○	○
5	○	○	○	○
6	○	○	○	○
7	○	○	○	○
8	○	○	○	○
9	○	○	○	○
10	○	○	○	○
11	○	○	○	○
12	○	○	○	○
13	○	○	○	○
14	○	○	○	○
15	○	○	○	○
16	○	○	○	○
17	○	○	○	○
18	○	○	○	○
19	○	○	○	○
20	○	○	○	○

Select the figure with the same relationship.

1. 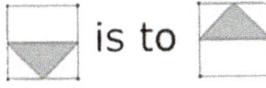 is to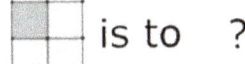

     is to ?

    a. 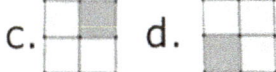 b.

    c. d.

2. 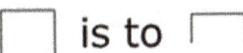 is to

    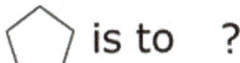 is to ?

    a. b.

    c. d.

3. 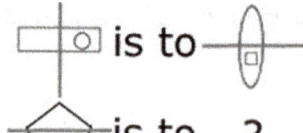 is to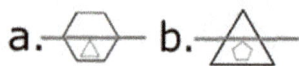

 is to ?

a. 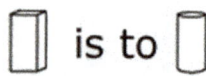 b.

c.  d.

4. is to

 is to ?

a. b.

c. d.

5.

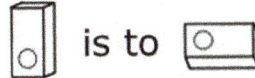

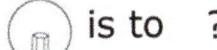

6.

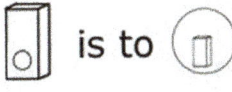

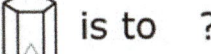

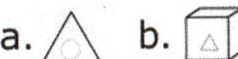

7.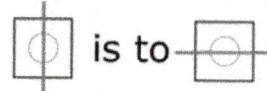

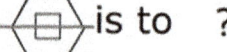 ?

a.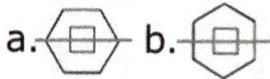

9.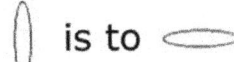

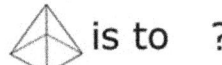

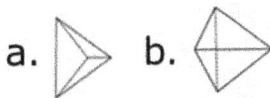

10.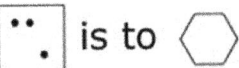

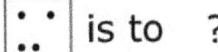

11. ☐ is to ⊡

△ is to ?

a. ⬠(•) b. △(:) c. △(•) d. ⬡(•)

12. ⊞(4 dots) is to ⊞(6 dots)

⊞(6 dots) is to ?

a. ⊞(4 dots) b. ⊞(6 dots) c. ⊞(3 dots) d. ⊞(4 dots)

13.

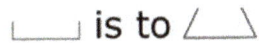 is to △

⊔⊔ is to ?

a. ⌒   b. ⌂

c. ⊔   d. △

14.

▫ is to ⌉

⬠ is to ?

a. ⟩   b. ⟩

c. ⟩   d. ⌉

15.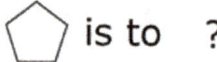

   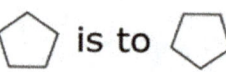

   a. ⟩   b. ⟩

   c. ⟩   d. ⏌

16. ⬠ is to ⬠

   △ is to ?

   a. ▽   b. ◁

   c. ▷   d. ⌷

17.

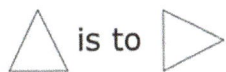

18.

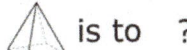

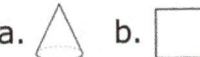

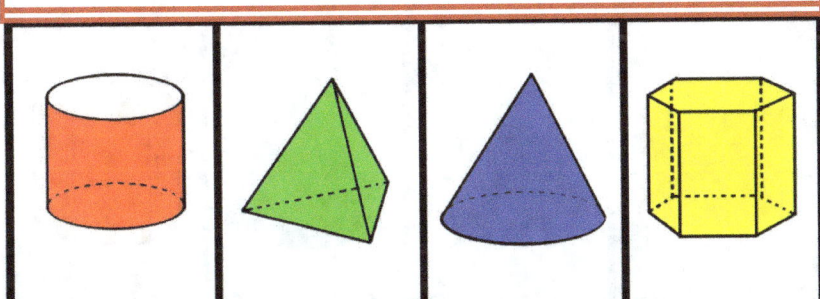

19. □ is to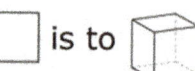

△ is to ?

a. △ b. △ (pyramid)

c. ⬠ d. (cylinder)

20. ⬠ is to ⬡

⬡ is to ?

a. □ b. ○

c. ⬠ d. ⬡

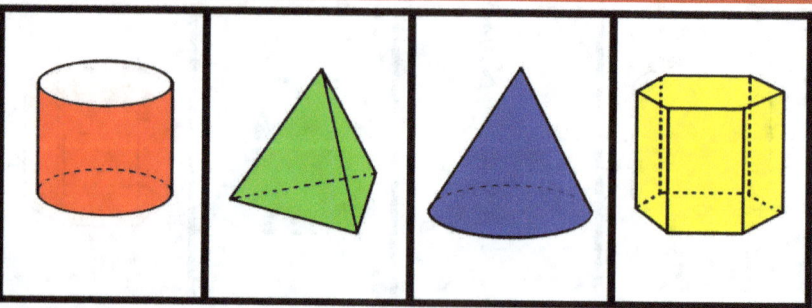

Answer Key

1. D
The relationship is the same figure flipped vertically, so the best choice is D.

2. C
The relation is the same figure with the bottom half removed.

3. D
The first pair is a rectangle with a circle inside and then an oval with a square inside. The given figures in the second pair has a triangle inside, so the match will be the circle with a square inside.

4. B
The relation is two upright figures in the first set, and 2 horizontal figures in the second set.

5. C
The first pair contains a box with a circle inside, and the same figure on its side.

6. C
The inside and larger shapes are reversed.

7. D
The relation is the same figure rotated.

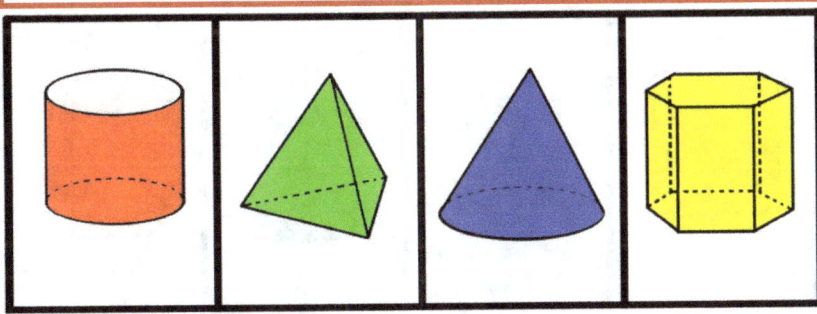

8. D
The larger figure has a smaller version inside.

9. D
The relation is the same figure rotated to the right.

10. B
The relation is the number of dots is one-half the number of sides.

11. C
The pattern is the same figure with a dot inside.

12. A
The figure rotates clockwise.

13. B
The relation is the bottom half of the figure.

14. C
The relation is the right half of the first object.

15. B
The relation is the right half of the first object.

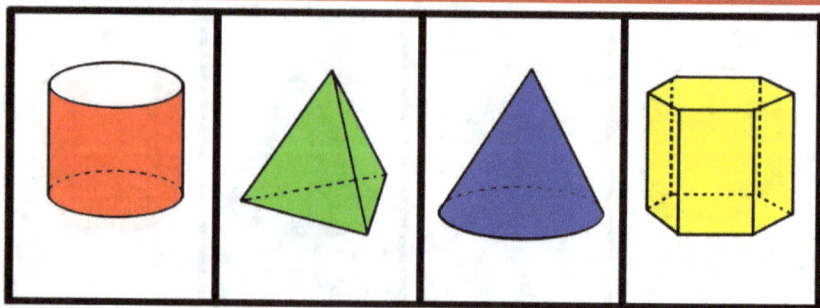

16. A
The relation is the same figure rotated.

17. D
The relation is the same figure rotated.

18. B
The relation is a 3-dimensional figure to a 2-dimensional figure.

19. B
The relation is a 2-dimensional figure to a 3-dimensional figure.

20. B
The relation is a n-sided figure to an n + 1 sided figure.

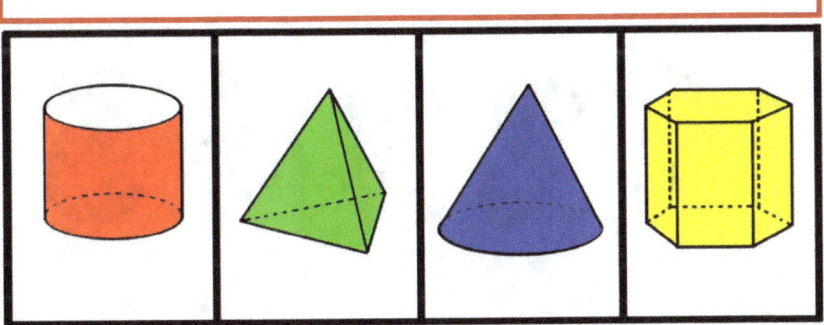

Number Analogies

The Number Analogies section assesses a child's ability to understand numerical relationships and patterns. This section is part of the quantitative reasoning skills tested in the CCAT, which are crucial for solving problems involving numbers and mathematical concepts.

In this section, children are presented with a series of number pairs that have a specific relationship. They are then asked to identify the number that completes a second pair, following the same relationship.

This skill is essential for developing strong mathematical reasoning and problem-solving abilities.

1. Understand the Relationship: Carefully examine the first pair of numbers to understand the relationship between them. It could be addition, subtraction, multiplication, division, or a more complex pattern.

2. Apply the Same Relationship: Once you identify the relationship in the first pair, apply the same relationship to the second pair to find the missing number.

3. Practice Basic Math Operations: Ensure you are comfortable with basic math operations like addition, subtraction, multiplication, and division, as these are commonly used in number analogies.

4. Look for Patterns: Sometimes, the relationship between numbers involves patterns, such as doubling, halving, or following a sequence. Recognize these patterns to solve the analogy.

5. Use Elimination: This is the best strategy for any multiple choice test. If you are unsure of the answer, use the process of elimination to narrow down the choices. Eliminate the options that do not fit the identified relationship.

6. Check Your Work: After selecting an answer, double-check to ensure that the relationship holds true for both pairs of numbers.

Quiz Answer Sheet

	A	B	C	D	E		A	B	C	D	E
1	○	○	○	○	○	21	○	○	○	○	○
2	○	○	○	○	○	22	○	○	○	○	○
3	○	○	○	○	○	23	○	○	○	○	○
4	○	○	○	○	○	24	○	○	○	○	○
5	○	○	○	○	○	25	○	○	○	○	○
6	○	○	○	○	○	26	○	○	○	○	○
7	○	○	○	○	○	27	○	○	○	○	○
8	○	○	○	○	○	28	○	○	○	○	○
9	○	○	○	○	○	29	○	○	○	○	○
10	○	○	○	○	○	30	○	○	○	○	○
11	○	○	○	○	○						
12	○	○	○	○	○						
13	○	○	○	○	○						
14	○	○	○	○	○						
15	○	○	○	○	○						
16	○	○	○	○	○						
17	○	○	○	○	○						
18	○	○	○	○	○						
19	○	○	○	○	○						
20	○	○	○	○	○						

Number Analogies

1. If 5 is like a thumb, what is like a pinky?

    a. 5   b. 1
    c. 10   d. 6

2. If 6 is like a cookie, what is like half a cookie?

    a. 3   b. 2
    c. 4   d. 12

3. If 10 is like a bag, what is like half the bag?

    a. 5   b. 15
    c. 20   d. 10

**4. Complete the number analogy:
3 is to 6 as 4 is to ?**

    a. 8   b. 10
    c. 6   d. 5

5. 20 is to 40 as 7 is to __.

    a. 10   b. 14
    c. 21   d. 28

6. Find the missing number in the analogy: 5 is to 25 as 7 is to ?

    a. 35   b. 49
    c. 18   d. 14

7. If 9 is to 3, then 15 is to ?

    a. 6   b. 4
    c. 5   d. 8

8. Choose the correct analogy:
12 is to dozen as 60 is to ?

    a. half dozen b. dozen

    c. five dozen d. two dozen

9. 5 is to 10 as 3 is to ___.

    a. 6   b. 9

    c. 12   d. 15

10. 9 is to 27 as 6 is to ___.

    a. 12   b. 18

    c. 24   d. 36

11. 15 is to 45 as 12 is to ___.

    a. 20   b. 24
    c. 36   d. 36

12. Complete the number analogy: 2 : 1 :: 8 : ?

    a. 2   b. 4
    c. 10   d. 12

13. Fill in the blank: 4 : 1/2 :: 40 : ?

    a. 2   b. 4
    c. 10   d. 5

14. What completes the analogy: 1 : 1/4 :: 8 : ?

    a. 1   b. 2
    c. 3   d. 4

15. Choose the correct answer:
10 : 5 :: 50 : ?

    a. 14   b. 25
    c. 20   d. 24

16. Find the missing number:
1/2 : 2 :: 1/4 : ?

    a. 4   b. 6
    c. 1   d. 12

17. 25 is to 15 as 50 is to __?

    a. 25   b. 30
    c. 35   d. 40

18. 3 is to 18 as 10 is to __?

    a. 60   b. 80
    c. 120   d. 150

19. 10 is to 1 as 30 is to __?

    a. 12   b. 9
    c. 3   d. 27

20. 2 is to 16 as 10 is to __?

    a. 20   b. 40
    c. 15   d. 80

21. 9 is to 27 as 15 is to __?

    a. 45   b. 38
    c. 36   d. 30

22. 25 is to 50 as 3 is to ?

    a. 5   b. 9
    c. 15   d. 6

Number Analogies

23. 3 is to 18 as 10 is to ?

    a. 50   b. 20
    c. 60   d. 30

24. 10 is to 2 as 20 is to ?

    a. 12   b. 8
    c. 16   d. 4

25. 2 is to 16 as 9 is to ?

    a. 12   b. 25
    c. 72   d. 27

26. 9 is to 27 as 25 is to ?

    a. 75   b. 50
    c. 30   d. 90

27. 20 is to 4 as 40 is to ?

    a. 5   b. 8
    c. 10   d. 6

28. 3 is to 9 as 5 is to ?

    a. 15   b. 10
    c. 3   d. 6

29. 1/2 is to 1/4 as 4 is to ?

    a. 2   b. 1
    c. 8   d. 16

30. 2 is to 50 as 5 is to ?

    a. 10   b. 12
    c. 125 d. 25

Answer Key

1. B
When you count fingers, the pinky comes next after the thumb. Hence, the answer is 1.

2. A
Half of a cookie would be like having only one part of the original cookie, which is 3.

3. A
Half of the bag would be like having only one part of the original bag, which is 5.

4. A
The analogy is based on doubling the initial number. So, 3 x 2 = 6, and similarly, 4 x 2 = 8.

5. B
The correct answer is 28. In this analogy, each number is multiplied by 2. So, 7 x 2 = 14.

6. A
This analogy involves squaring the initial number. 5 X 5 = 25, and 7 X 5 = 35.

7. C
In this analogy, the initial number is divided by 3 to get the result. 9 / 3 = 3. Following the same pattern, 15 / 3 = 5.

8. C
A dozen represents 12, so five dozen would be 5 x 12 = 60.

9. A
The correct answer is 6. In this analogy, each number is multiplied by 2. So, 3 x 2 = 6.

10. B
The correct answer is 18. In this analogy, each number is multiplied by 3. So, 6 x 3 = 18.

11. C
The correct answer is 36. In this analogy, each number is multiplied by 3. So, 12 x 3 = 36.

12. B
The pattern is: 2 / 2 = 1. Therefore, 8 / 2 = 4.

13. D
The relation is: 4 / 8 = 1/2. So, 40 / 8 = 5.

14. B
Following the pattern: 1 / 4 = 1/4. So, 8 x 1/4 = 2.

15. B
By applying the pattern: 10 / 2 = 5. Then, 50 / 2 = 25.

16. C
The relationship is: 1/2 x 4 = 2. Thus, 1/4 x 4 = 1.

17. D
In the first pair, 15 is 10 less than 25. Applying the same logic to the second pair, 40 is 10 less than 50.

18. A
The relationship between 3 and 18 is 6 times. Following this pattern, 10 times 6 equals 60.

19. C
In the given analogy, 1 is 10 / 10 . Following the same logic, 30 / 10 is 3.

20. D
In the initial pair, 2 X 8 is 16. Applying the same ratio, 10 is 8 times less than 80.

21. A
The relation between 9 and 27 is that 27 is 3 times 9. Following this pattern, 15 times 3 equals 45.

22. D
The correct answer is 6. This analogy follows the pattern of multiplying the first number by 2 to get the second number.

23. C
The correct answer is 60. This analogy follows the pattern of multiplying the first number by 6 to get the second number.

24. D
The correct answer is 4. This analogy follows the pattern of dividing the first number by 5 to get the second number.

25. C
The correct answer is 72. This analogy follows the pattern of multiplying the first number by 8 to get the second number.

26. A
The correct answer is 75. This analogy follows the pattern of multiplying the first number by 3 to get the second number.

27. B
The relationship between 20 and 4 is division by 5 (20 ÷ 5 = 4). Following the same pattern, 40 ÷ 5 = 8.

28. A
The relationship between 3 and 9 is multiplication by 3 (3 x 3 = 9). Following the same pattern, 5 x 3 = 15.

29. A
The relationship between 1/2 and 1/4 is division by 2 (1/2 ÷ 2 = 1/4). Following the same pattern, 4 ÷ 2 = 2.

30. C
The relationship between 2 and 50 is multiplication by 25 (2 x 25 = 50). Following the same pattern, 5 x 25 = 125.

Number Series

The CCAT Number Series section evaluates your ability to identify patterns and logical rules in sequences of numbers or letters. In this section, you will be presented with a series of numbers or letters and your task is to determine the next item in the sequence based on the pattern.

This section tests your numerical reasoning skills and your ability to quickly recognize and apply mathematical rule

How to Answer Number Series Questions

1. First, Identify the Pattern: Look for common patterns such as addition, subtraction, multiplication, division, or a combination of these. Sometimes the pattern might involve alternating sequences or more complex mathematical operations.

2. Write Down Differences: If the pattern isn't immediately obvious, write down the differences between consecutive numbers. This can help you spot a consistent change or pattern.

3. Familiarize with Common Patterns: The practice questions below will help you to recognize common number series patterns, such as arithmetic sequences (where the difference between numbers is constant), geometric sequences (where each number is multiplied by a constant), and others.

4. Use Elimination: This is the most powerful multiple choice strategy for any test. Rule out unlikely options. This can help narrow down the possible answers.

Answer Sheet

	A	B	C	D
1	○	○	○	○
2	○	○	○	○
3	○	○	○	○
4	○	○	○	○
5	○	○	○	○
6	○	○	○	○
7	○	○	○	○
8	○	○	○	○
9	○	○	○	○
10	○	○	○	○
11	○	○	○	○
12	○	○	○	○
13	○	○	○	○
14	○	○	○	○
15	○	○	○	○
16	○	○	○	○
17	○	○	○	○
18	○	○	○	○
19	○	○	○	○
20	○	○	○	○

Quiz 1

1. Consider the following sequence: 6, 12, 24, 48, ... What number should come next?

    a. 48   b. 64

    c. 60   d. 96

2. Consider the following sequence: 5, 6, 11, 17, ... What number should come next?

    a. 28   b. 34

    c. 36   d. 27

3. Consider the following sequence: 26, 21, ..., 11, 6. What is the missing number?

   a. 27   b. 23

   c. 16   d. 29

4. Consider the following sequence: L, O, R, ..., Y What is the missing letter?

   a. S   b. U

   c. T   d. M

5. Consider the following sequence: X, Z, B, D, ... What number should come next?

    a. E   b. F

    c. G   d. H

6. Consider the sequence in row A compared to row B. What is the missing number?

A	5	20	100	3	24
B	20	80	400	12	?

    a. 96   b. 48

    c. 64   d. 66

7. Consider the following sequence: L, N, P, R, ... What letter should come next?

    a. S   b. T

    c. U   d. V

8. Consider the following sequence: M, P, S, , Y. What is the missing letter?

    a. V   b. T

    c. U   d. X

9. Consider the following sequence:

      ???

a.    b.    c.

10. Consider the following sequence:

+ * + * | * + * + | * * + * | + + __ __

    a. + *   b. * *
    c. + +   d. * +

11. Consider the following sequence: 64, 50, 38, 28, 20, ... Find the first three terms.

    a. 15, 10, 5   b. 14, 10, 8
    c. 10, 0, -10   d. 12, 4, -6

12. 2 4 8 16 | 5 10 20 40 | 4 8 16 32 | 3 6 ... 24

    a. 4   b. 12
    c. 8   d. 10

13. Consider the following sequence: 10, 13, 16, 19, ...   What 3 numbers should come next?

    a. 21, 23, 25   b. 21, 24, 27
    c. 22, 25, 28   d. 23, 26, 29

14. Consider Box A and the relationship to the numbers in Box B. What is the missing number in Box B?

Box A

8	12
5	9

Box B

19	27
13	?

a. 18 b. 21
c. 24 d. 14

15. Consider the following sequence: 8, 11, 9, 12, 10, 13, ... What number should come next?

    a. 11   b. 10
    c. 15   d. 16

16. Consider the following sequence: 2, 1, (1/2), (1/4), ... What number should come next?

    a. 1/3   b. 1/8
    c. 1/16   d. 2/8

17. Consider the following sequence: 10, 20, 40, 80, ... What number should come next?

    a. 150   b. 120
    c. 90   d. 160

18. Consider the following sequence: 18395, 18295, 18195, 18095, ... What number should come next?

    a. 18000   b. 18950
    c. 17995   d. 17905

19. Consider the following sequence: -45, -39, -33, -27, ... What number should come next?

    a. 21   b. -21
    c. -25   d. 25

20. Consider the following sequence: ..., ..., 20, 32, 44, 56, 68. Find the first two terms.

    a. -4, 8   b. 0, 12
    c. -6, 8   d. 2, 8

Answer Key

1. D
The numbers doubles each time.

2. A
Each number is the sum of the previous two numbers

3. C
The numbers decrease by 5 each time.

4. B
There are two letters missing between each one, so U is next.

5. B
Miss a letter each time and 'loop' back, so F is next.

6. A
The number in row B is 4 times the number in row A.

7. B
One letter is missing after each letter.

8. A
Two letters are missing after each letter.

9. B
The sequence shifts to the left each time, so the next figure will be the circle.

10. D
Each time the * and + alternate, either singly or doubles.

11. B
The sequence decreases by 2 less each time.
64 --> 50   14
50 -> 38   12
38 -> 28   10
28 -> 20   8
20 --> 14   6
14 -> 10   4

12. B
The numbers double each time.

13. B
The number increase by 3 each time

14. B
The numbers in Box B are the result of (number in Box A * 2)+ 3. So the missing number is 21.

15. A
The sequence increases initially and then decreases in the next term. The relationship between each increase is +3 and the relationship with the alternate decrease is -3. So the answer is -2 from the last given term. 13 – 2 = 11.

16. B
The sequence is decreasing by half. So half of 1/4 = 1/8

17. D
The sequence is increasing. Each new term is obtained by multiplying the last term by 2. Therefore, 80 x 2 = 160

18. C
Each new term is calculated by subtracting 100 from the last term. So, 18095 – 100 = 17995

19. B
Each new term is calculated by adding 6 to the last term, therefore, -27 + 6 = -21

20. A
The sequence is increasing by 12. To find first two terms, we solve backwards by subtracting 12.

NUMBER SERIES QUIZ 2
ANSWER SHEET

	A	B	C	D
1	○	○	○	○
2	○	○	○	○
3	○	○	○	○
4	○	○	○	○
5	○	○	○	○
6	○	○	○	○
7	○	○	○	○
8	○	○	○	○
9	○	○	○	○
10	○	○	○	○
11	○	○	○	○
12	○	○	○	○
13	○	○	○	○
14	○	○	○	○
15	○	○	○	○
16	○	○	○	○
17	○	○	○	○
18	○	○	○	○
19	○	○	○	○
20	○	○	○	○

1. Consider the following sequence: 3, 5, 10, 12, 24, ... What 2 numbers should come next?

    a. 48, 58   b. 26, 28

    c. 48, 50   d. 26, 52

2. Consider the following sequence: 1000, 992, 984, 976, ... What 2 numbers should come next?

    a. 968, 961   b. 967, 960

    c. 968, 960   d. 970, 964

3. Consider the following sequence: 0.1, 0.3, 0.9, 2.7, ... What 2 numbers should come next?

    a. -8.1, -24.3   b. 8.1, 24.3

    c. 5.4, 10.8   d. -5.4, -10.8

4. Consider the following sequence: 32, 16, 8, 4, ... What 3 numbers should come next?

    a. 2, 1, 0.5   b. 2, 0, -2

    c. 0, -4, -8   d. 2, 1, 0

5. Consider the following sequence: 3, ..., 9, 12, 15. What is the missing number?

    a. 4   b. 7

    c. 6   d. 5

6. Consider the following sequence: 1132, 1121, ... , 1199, ... What number comes next?

    a. 1109   b. 1188

    c. 1189   d. 1180

7. Consider the following sequence: 95, 90, ..., 80, 75. What is the missing number?

    a. 87   b. 85

    c. 86   d. 80

8. Consider the following sequence: ..., 75, 65, 60, 50, 45, 35, ... What 2 numbers are missing?

    a. 70, 35   b. 65, 35

    c. 80, 30   d. 65, 30

9. Consider the following sequence: 91, 85, ..., ..., 67, 61. What 2 numbers are missing?

    a. 81, 71   b. 78, 72

    c. 80, 70   d. 79, 73

10. Consider the following sequence: ..., ..., 120, 129, 138, 147. Find the first two terms.

    a. 102, 111   b. 100, 110

    c. 102, 112   d. 99, 111

11. Consider the following sequence: ..., 95, 88, 93, 86, 91, ... What 2 numbers are missing?

    a. 88, 98   b. 90, 98

    c. 100, 84   d. 90, 84

12. Consider the following sequence: 76, 64, 54, 46, ..., 36, ..., . What 2 numbers are missing?

    a. 40, 32   b. 40, 34

    c. 42, 30   d. 42, 32

13. Consider the following sequence: 3, ..., 12, ..., 48, 96. What 2 numbers are missing?

    a. 6, 36   b. 6, 18

    c. 8, 16   d. 6, 24

14. Consider the following sequence: 3, 13, 22, 30, 37, ... What number comes next?

    a. 45   b. 47

    c. 43   d. 42

15. Consider the following sequence: ..., ..., 4, 9, 14, 19. Find the first two terms.

    a. -5, 0   b. 0, 2

    c. -6,-1   d. -5, 0

16. Consider the following sequence: 63, 57, 52, 48, ... What number comes next?

    a. 42   b. 37

    c. 45   d. 40

17. Consider the following sequence: 17, 23, 29, 35, ... What 3 numbers should come next?

    a. 41, 47, 54
    b. 42, 47, 53
    c. 40, 45, 50
    d. 41, 47, 53

18. Consider the following sequence: 11, 15, 20, 26, ... What 3 numbers should come next?

    a. 31, 37, 42
    b. 33, 41, 50
    c. 32, 38, 46
    d. 36, 46, 56

19. Consider the following sequence: 45, 40, ..., 30, 25. What is the missing number?

    a. 35   b. 38

    c. 33   d. 32

20. Consider the following sequence: 120, 110, ..., 90, 80. What is the missing number?

    a. 95   b. 100

    c. 105   d. 115

Answer Key

1. D
The sequence is increasing by adding 2 and multiplying 2 alternately. The next 2 terms are 24 + 2= 26 and 26 x 2 = 52.

2. C
The sequence is decreasing by 8.

3. B
The sequence is increasing by multiplying each the last term by 3. 2.7 x 3= 8.1 and 8.1 x 3 = 24.3

4. A
The sequence is decreasing by dividing the last term by 2.

5. C
The sequence is increasing by +3.

6. B
The sequence is reducing by 11.

7. B
The sequence is decreasing by +5.

8. C
The sequence is decreasing by -5 and -10 alternately; the first term is 75 – 5 = 70 and the last term is 35 – 10= 30.

9. D
The sequence is increasing by +6.

10. A
The sequence is increasing by +9.

11. D
The sequence is increasing and decreasing alternately. It increases by +5 and decreases by -7. The first term will thus be the second term 95 – 5 = 90 and the last term will be 91 – 7 = 84.

12. B
The difference between the terms starts from 12 and decreases by 2 i.e. 12, 10,8,6,4,2. The missing terms are 46 – 6=40 and 34 – 0 =34

13. D
Each term is being doubled or multiplied by 2 to get the next term. 3 x 2 = 6 and 12 x 2 = 24.

14. C
The sequence increase by 1 less each time.
3 + 10 = 13
13 + 9 = 22
22 + 8 = 30
30+ 7 = 37

15. D
The sequence increases by 5 each time.

16. C
The sequence decreases by 1 less each time
63 - 6 = 57
57 - 5 = 52
52 - 4 = 48

17. D
The sequence increases by 6 each time.

18. B
The sequence increases by +1 each time
11 + 4 = 15
15 + 5 = 20
20 + 6 = 26
26 + 7 = 33
33 + 8 = 41
41 + 9 = 50

19. A
The sequence decreases by 5 each time. So, the missing number is 45 - 5 - 5 = 35.

20. B
The sequence decreases by 10 each time. So, the missing number is 120 - 10 - 10 = 100.

Number Puzzles

In this section, students are presented with a puzzles that involve numbers and simple equations, where one item is missing.

Number puzzles help young learners develop their mathematical thinking in a fun and interactive way.

Answer Sheet

	A	B	C	D	E		A	B	C	D	E
1	○	○	○	○	○	21	○	○	○	○	○
2	○	○	○	○	○	22	○	○	○	○	○
3	○	○	○	○	○	23	○	○	○	○	○
4	○	○	○	○	○	24	○	○	○	○	○
5	○	○	○	○	○	25	○	○	○	○	○
6	○	○	○	○	○						
7	○	○	○	○	○						
8	○	○	○	○	○						
9	○	○	○	○	○						
10	○	○	○	○	○						
11	○	○	○	○	○						
12	○	○	○	○	○						
13	○	○	○	○	○						
14	○	○	○	○	○						
15	○	○	○	○	○						
16	○	○	○	○	○						
17	○	○	○	○	○						
18	○	○	○	○	○						
19	○	○	○	○	○						
20	○	○	○	○	○						

1. 2 + ___ = 9

    a. 7   b. 3

    c. 6   d. 8

2. (3 X 4) − 5 = ___

    a. 17   b. 7

    c. 12   d. 15

3. (8 X 2) X (2 X 3) = ___

    a. 60   b. 72

    c. 96   d. 92

4. ___ + (6 * 7) = 43

    a. 5   b. 2

    c. 9   d. 1

5. 7 + (3 X ___) = 28

    a. 7   b. 4

    c. 6   d. 10

6. 8 - ? = 3

    a. 2   b. 3

    c. 5   d. 8

7. What number is missing in the equation: 5 + ? = 12?

    a. 3   b. 6

    c. 7   d. 8

8. What number is missing in the equation: 9 - ? = 3?

    a. 4   b. 5

    c. 6   d. 7

9. What number is missing in the equation: 4 x ? = 16?

    a. 2   b. 3

    c. 4   d. 5

10. What number is missing in the equation: 14 ÷ ? = 7?

    a. 1   b. 2

    c. 3   d. 4

11. What number is missing in the equation: 10 + ? = 15?

    a. 3   b. 4

    c. 5   d. 6

12. 4 x ? = 16

    a. 2   b. 4

    c. 6   d. 8

13. 12 ÷ ? = 3

    a. 2   b. 3

    c. 4   d. 6

14. ? + 7 = 15

    a. 6   b. 8

    c. 9   d. 10

15. If 5 + ? = 8, what is the missing number?

    a. 2   b. 3

    c. 4   d. 5

16. If 10 - ? = 6, what is the missing number?

    a. 3   b. 4

    c. 6   d. 8

17. Complete the pattern: 2, 4, 6, ?, 10

    a. 7   b. 8

    c. 9   d. 11

18. If 18 ÷ ? = 3, what is the missing number?

    a. 3   b. 4

    c. 5   d. 6

**19. What number completes the equation:
5 + ? = 12?**

    a. 4   b. 6

    c. 7   d. 8

20. What is the missing number in the equation: 15 - ? = 9?

    a. 4   b. 5

    c. 6   d. 7

21. What number is missing in the equation: 8 x ? = 32?

    a. 3   b. 4

    c. 5   d. 6

22. Complete the equation: ? ÷ 4 = 5

    a. 15   b. 16

    c. 17   d. 18

23. Find the missing number: 27 / ? = 9

    a. 2   b. 3

    c. 4   d. 5

24. If 8 - ? = 3, what should replace the question mark?

    a. 4   b. 5

    c. 6   d. 7

25. What is the missing number in the equation: 6 x 3 = ?

    a. 12   b. 15

    c. 18   d. 21

Answer Key

1. A
2. B
3. B
4. D
5. A
6. A
7. D
8. B
9. C
10. A
11. C
12. D
13. B
14. C
15. B
16. B
17. A
18. C
19. C
20. A
21. B
22. A
23. B
24. A
25. B

After Taking a Practice Test

What to do after you take a practice test

- Go through your answers carefully. For each wrong answer, refer to the explanation, and work through the questions step-by-step.

- What kind of question (e.g. analogies, sentence completion etc.)

- Look for patterns in your incorrect answers – what is it exactly that you are doing wrong or don't understand.

- What types of questions do you have the most difficulty with? Refer to the tutorials and try to understand the questions.

Getting the Most from Practice Questions

Taking a practice test is probably the best way to prepare for a test.

Quick tips to get the most from practice questions:

Simulate Test Conditions

- Choose a quiet, distraction-free environment.

- Use a timer and allow just under 1 minute per question.

- Avoid using notes or online texts while doing practice questions

Take it seriously -

- Treat the practice test as if it's the real exam

- Familiarize yourself with the format and topics - this will reduce anxiety.

Practice questions come in varying degrees of difficulty, ranging from basic to advanced levels.

This diversity helps in assessing different aspects of your understanding and skills. To handle these effectively, start by thoroughly reading each question to understand what is being asked. For easier questions, focus on accuracy and speed. For more challenging ones, break them down into smaller parts and tackle each part methodically.

Remember, staying calm and confident is key to successfully navigating through questions of all difficulty levels.

After Completing a Practice Test

Reviewing your work after you take a practice test is critical.

Immediate Review

- Make a note of any questions you found challenging or topics that felt unfamiliar or difficult.

- How was your time management?

- Overall comfort during the test?

Do a Thorough Review

- Go over your answers focusing on correct and incorrect answers.

- For incorrect answers, identify misunderstandings knowledge gaps or problem subject areas - here is where you need to spend your study time.

- **Look for Patterns**

- Look for recurring themes in your errors to pinpoint specific areas needing improvement.

- Assess whether mistakes were due to content gaps, misinterpretation of questions, or time constraints.

Test Preparation Tips

1. Create a Study Schedule:
Set aside a specific time each day for studying. For example, study for 30 minutes after school every day.

2. Use Flashcards:
Write down key facts or vocabulary words on flashcards. Review them regularly.

3. Take Breaks:
Take short breaks during study sessions to stay focused. For example, study for 20 minutes, then take a 5-minute break to stretch or have a snack.

4. Get a Good Night's Sleep:
Make sure to get plenty of rest the night before the test. For example, go to bed early to ensure you are well-rested and alert.

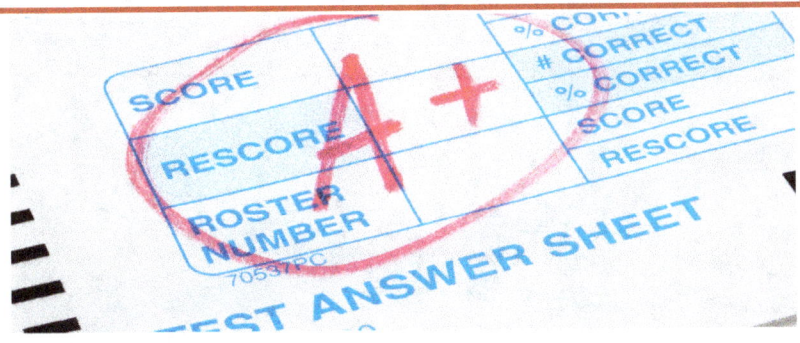

5. Stay Positive and Confident:
Think positive and be confident. For example, remind yourself that you have studied and are prepared for the test.

6. Ask for Help:
If you don't understand something, ask a teacher, parent, or friend for help.

How to Answer Multiple Choice

1. Read the Question Carefully:
Make sure to read the entire question before looking at the answer choices. For example, if the question asks, "What is 5 + 3?" make sure you understand it is asking for the sum of 5 and 3.

2. Look at All the Answer Choices:
Read all the answer choices before selecting one. For example, if the choices are 6, 7, 8, and 9, make sure to consider each one before choosing.

3. Eliminate Wrong Answers:
Cross out the answers you know are incorrect. For example, if you know 5 + 3 is not 6 or 7, eliminate those choices.

4. Use Process of Elimination:
Narrow down your choices by eliminating the wrong answers. For example, if you are left with 8 and 9, think about which one makes the most sense.

5. Look for Clues in the Question:
Sometimes the question itself can give you hints about the correct answer. For example, if the question asks about a "sum," you know it is asking for an addition problem.

6. Double-Check Your Work:
If you have time, go back and review your answers. For example, make sure you didn't make a simple mistake like adding incorrectly.

7. Stay Calm and Focused:
Take deep breaths and stay calm. For example, if you feel nervous, take a moment to relax before answering the next question.

8. Trust Your First Instinct:

Often, your first choice is the correct one. For example, if you initially think the answer is 8, go with that unless you find a reason to change it.

9. Don't Leave Any Questions Blank:
If you are unsure, make your best guess. For example, if you don't know the answer, choose the one that seems most likely.

Conclusion

Congratulations! You have made it this far because you have applied yourself diligently to practicing for the exam and no doubt improved your potential score considerably! Getting into a good school is a huge step in a journey that might be challenging at times but will be many times more rewarding and fulfilling. That is why being prepared is so important.

Study then Practice and then Succeed!

Good Luck!

www.ingramcontent.com/pod-product-compliance
Lightning Source LLC
Chambersburg PA
CBHW072155070526
44585CB00015B/1144